Milksnakes

FROM THE EXPERTS AT
ADVANCED VIVARIUM SYSTEMS®

Bryan Engler with Jerry Walls

THE HERPETOCULTURAL LIBRARY®

Andrew DePrisco, June Kikuchi, *Editorial Directors*
Jarelle S. Stein, *Editor*
Jennifer Calvert, *Associate Editor*
Elizabeth Spurbeck, *Assistant Editor*
Cindy Kassebaum, *Art Director*
Karen Julian, *Publishing Coordinator*
Tracy Burns, *Production Coordinator*
Jessica Jaensch, *Production Coordinator*
Melody Englund, *Indexer*

Thank you to Russ Case, Group Editor of *REPTILES* magazine, for reviewing the manuscript.

Cover photograph by Dave Northcott.

The photographs in this book are courtesy of **Kevin Collison:** pp. 5, 42, 46, 60, 64, 70, 73 (top), 85, 87, 90; **Isabelle Francais:** pp. 9, 28, 36, 50, 52, 57, 62, 80, 81, 83, 106; **Paul Freed:** p. 116; **Zig Leszczynski:** p. 68; **Bill Love:** pp. 11, 20, 34, 94, 99, 110, 112, 114; **Gerold Merker:** pp. 56, 65, 69, 71, 72, 74, 75, 78; **John Rossi:** pp. 39, 44, 104; **Amy B. Scully:** p. 77; **Maleta M. Walls:** pp. 25, 48, 54, 67, 70, 102, 118; **W. P. Mara:** pp. 7, 18, 26, 30, 35, 66, 73 (bottom), 97.

LCCN: 96-183295
ISBN-10: 1-882770-98-6
ISBN-13: 978-1-882770-98-4

An Imprint of BowTie Press®
A Division of BowTie, Inc.
3 Burroughs
Irvine, California 92618
www.avsbooks.com

Printed and bound in China
14 13 12 11 10 1 2 3 4 5 6 7 8 9 10

Contents

Introduction

The science of the study of reptiles and amphibians is known as *herpetology*, and someone who studies reptiles and amphibians is a *herpetologist*. Hobbyists have altered these terms quite a bit. Today a *herp* is any reptile or amphibian, *herping* is collecting or looking for herps, and *herpetoculture* is taking care of herps. Someone who is interested in herps is a *herper*. Although some purists object to these terms, they are here to stay, and you will find them used everywhere in herp literature.

The hobby of keeping and breeding reptiles and amphibians has enjoyed tremendous growth over the past two decades. Among all of the herps, snakes are by far the most popular and the most beloved of keepers, especially of relatively advanced hobbyists. More than 3,000 snake species exist worldwide. Interestingly, however, fewer than 5 percent (which would be 150 species, for those who don't feel like doing the math) are commonly kept as pets. That's a fairly exclusive group, wouldn't you say? Kind of a serpentine country club, comprising the cream of the crop, as it were.

The book you're holding is about one member of that elite fraternity—the milksnake. Milksnakes belong to the genus *Lampropeltis* (the kingsnakes) and the species *triangulum*. (Confused by the Latin names? Don't worry—I'll give you a key to understanding them a bit later.) Milksnakes are found exclusively in the Americas and have one of the largest ranges (area where they are found naturally) of any species of snake. Bred by the thousands, these snakes now exist in myriad "designer" varieties, such as albino, reduced black, and even nearly solid red. In fact, their evolution in the pet trade has in many ways exceeded their evolution in nature, with far more color varieties in the terrarium than in nature. It certainly would be safe to say they rank among the most popular of all pet snakes.

Albino snakes such as these baby Nelson's milksnakes are popular among herpers because of their vibrant coloring.

I hope that this book will provide the information necessary to make you as knowledgeable and efficient a milksnake keeper as possible. Happily, the captive care of the milksnake is not a particularly difficult endeavor. Milksnakes breed readily, are hardy, take particular delight in feeding, and are almost always amenable to human interaction. And, of course, they are beautiful. Sleek, modest in size (3 or 4 feet for the largest forms), and strikingly patterned, usually with rings of red, black, and yellow or white, they may capture the admiration of even an ophidiophobe (a person who fears snakes). A moment's reflection makes it easy to understand how the milksnake, in all its varieties, attained its lofty status.

After you've finished reading this book, look around to find more detailed information to further your knowledge. Articles on breeding many unique subspecies and color forms have been published in reptile magazines. The Internet is filled with photos and information, including details from successful breeders. Absorb as much knowledge as you can— you'll be able to use all of it. So set your goals high, and be the best keeper you can be! Your pets are depending on you.

CHAPTER 1

Milksnake Classification

L et's begin our study of milksnakes by clarifying some key points concerning their many names. Most animal and plant species have two types of names: scientific and common. Scientific names are given to animals and plants by taxonomists (the scientists who identify and describe them) and are often based on Latin, the language of scientists for several hundred years. That's why scientific names are sometimes called Latin names. However, Greek, Arabic, some African and South American Indian dialects, and many other languages have now been widely incorporated into the scientific naming system.

Since the scientific appellations can be difficult in everyday

Why Milksnake?

How did this species acquire the common name milksnake? The answer lies in the habits of the subspecies from the northeastern United States, *Lampropeltis triangulum triangulum*. This brown subspecies was often found around barns in the colonies, where it fed on mice of various types. A legend developed that the snake actually fed on cow's milk, wrapping around the hind leg of a cow and sucking milk directly from the udder. Of course, this legend is nonsense (no cow would ever stand still for the bite of dozens of tiny snake teeth), but it still serves as the basis for the common name—and some people probably believe the legend to this day. By the way, the name *kingsnake* comes from early observations of the common kingsnake's killing and eating rattlesnakes and other venomous snakes, obviously making it the "king of all the snakes."

Lampropeltis triangulum campbelli **(Pueblan milksnake).**

usage, ordinary people (that is, we who are not taxonomists) have created simpler names—common names or nicknames—for the animals and plants we see around us. Besides, even if herpetology hobbyists know the scientific names for reptiles and amphibians, their "non-herp" friends probably do not. Imagine the confusion that would ensue if you told a non-herp friend that you just bought a new *Lampropeltis triangulum syspila*! He will probably have a better idea of what you're talking about if you were to refer to your new pet as a red milksnake.

The problem with common names, and the reason many taxonomists do not like them, is that they can be imprecise and misleading. For example, more than one serpent bears the common name of milksnake. So saying "I have a milksnake" does not reveal the whole picture. If, however, you said, "I have a *Lampropeltis triangulum syspila*," then you'd be telling someone in the know exactly what snake you have. That's the value of the scientific names—precision.

Binomial Nomenclature

The system for giving an animal a scientific name is called *binomial nomenclature*. This term essentially means "names with two names," and that's just what an animal receives through this process—a scientific name of two parts. The first part, which is always capitalized, is the generic name (the genus), and the second, which never is capitalized, is the specific name (the species). Take, for example, the scientific name *Lampropeltis triangulum*. *Lampropeltis* is the genus of all kingsnakes, of which there are at least ten species, including the milksnakes. The second part of the name, *triangulum*, is the name of a distinct kingsnake species, the milksnake proper. The next level beneath species, called subspecies, is used when even more specificity is necessary. Not all species have subspecies within them, but the milksnake does, as in *Lampropeltis triangulum syspila* (red milksnake) or *Lampropeltis triangulum gaigeae* (black milksnake). Often the genus and species names are abbreviated after they have been used once, so *Lampropeltis triangulum* could be written as *L. triangulum* and *Lampropeltis triangulum gaigeae* could be given as *L. t. gaigeae*. The genus (adj. generic), species (adj. specific), and subspecies (adj. subspecific) parts of a name are always set off from the type around them when written, usually by being underlined or italicized.

Technically, the scientific name also includes two other parts, the name of the describer of the species and the year in which he or she described it. *Lampropeltis triangulum* was described by a French scientist, the Comte de Lacépède, in 1788. Thus formally, the full scientific name of the milksnake is *Lampropeltis triangulum* (Lacépède, 1788). The parentheses around the describer and date indicate that the species was originally described in a genus other than the one in which it is currently placed. In this case, Lacépède, in 1788, placed the milksnake in the genus *Coluber*, classifying it as *Coluber triangulum*—today, as noted above, the milksnake resides in the genus *Lampropeltis* (kingsnake), with the specific classification *Lampropeltis triangulum*. The system of binomial nomenclature is some 250 years old, and it has been modified many times over since its inception. The basic system arose from the work of Swedish botanist Karl von Linne, who made the first practical attempt to describe and name all the plants and animals known to Europeans in the mid-eighteenth century. Linne, who wrote in Latin as Carolus Linnaeus, arranged all living things known to him in groups by obvious physical characters and then finely tuned the larger groups into smaller and smaller groups. The smallest groups

Lampropeltis triangulum sinaloae (Sinaloan milksnake).

were given names as species, while slightly larger groups were named as genera. In 1758, Linnaeus published a landmark volume that gave generic and specific names to all the animals then known to him, which at the time did not include any of the American kingsnakes. He did not formally describe our common kingsnake until eight years later, in 1766, when he assigned it the name *Coluber getulus*. The common kingsnake has now been reclassified, so its full scientific name is *Lampropeltis getula* (Linnaeus, 1766). The genus *Lampropeltis* (meaning something like "shining shields," in reference to the glossy scales) itself was first named in 1843 by the European herpetologist Leopold Fitzinger, who described many common snake genera.

Taxonomy

While the process of assigning proper scientific names to an animal is called nomenclature, the process of arranging and categorizing animals themselves is called taxonomy. Taxonomy isn't as complicated as you might think; it's just a system of organization. Taxonomists spend their time wondering, "Where does this one belong?" and "How do we tell these two apart?"

  In the most basic terms, the structure of the taxonomic

Lampropeltis doliata

If you look in the scientific literature before about 1970, you are likely to be puzzled by seeing the milksnake called by the scientific name *Lampropeltis doliata* (Linnaeus, 1766). What happened here? It seems that when Swedish scientist Carolus Linnaeus described this snake using a specimen he received from South Carolina, his description was so general that the name could be applied either to what is now called the scarlet snake, *Cemophora coccinea*, or to the scarlet kingsnake, *L. triangulum elapsoides*. In 1967, the name *doliata* was officially designated as a synonym for the scarlet snake, and the milksnake took the name *L. triangulum*.

system is a very special hierarchy of groups. At the top of the hierarchy is the kingdom (plants, animals, fungi, and so on), with the phylum—Annelida (segmented worms), Arthropoda (insects, crustaceans, and spiders), and Chordata (all vertebrate animals)—just below. Scientists recognize from two (Plantae, Animalia) to five kingdoms (add fungi, bacteria, and monerans) and from twenty to forty or so animal phyla—these are very large groups. At the opposite end of the hierarchy are the species and subspecies, the lowest levels of variation given formal names. There are probably well over a million species of animals living today, 75 percent of them beetles, with ants and some other insects not far behind.

Until recently, taxonomists had to basically depend on visible characteristics to name species and try to determine how they were related to each other. During the past twenty years or so, the powerful new tool of molecular genetics (looking in detail at the DNA making up the genes) has become available, making taxonomy a bit more accurate. Although the use of DNA and related molecular genetic characters is still in development, it is allowing snakes and all other living things to be viewed in a quite different way, looking beneath the skin, as it were. Not surprisingly, this is leading to changes in the names of familiar species and how they are categorized as relating to each other.

Although milksnakes, specifically, have not yet been studied in detail using molecular genetics, scientists are now fairly sure about where kingsnakes (*Lampropeltis*) the genus group to which the milks belong, generally fit into the scheme of things. The kingsnakes fall into a very distinctive group of strictly American snakes called the tribe Lampropeltini of the family Colubridae. Within this tribe also are the closely related snakes known as the American rat snakes (formerly called the genus *Elaphe* but now being split into five genera for American species—*Scotophis* for the rat snakes proper, *Pantherophis* for the corn snakes, and *Mintonius* for the fox snakes, as well as *Bogertophis* and perhaps *Pseudelaphe* for related species), the pine, gopher, and bull snakes (genus *Pituophis*), and a group of small relatives known as the genera *Stilosoma* (short-tailed snakes), *Arizona* (glossy snakes), *Cemophora* (scarlet snakes), and *Rhinocheilus* (long-nosed snakes).

New work on the molecular genetics of Lampropeltini shows that the short-tailed snakes, genus *Stilosoma*, are actually modified kingsnakes, perhaps related to the common kingsnake, and now to be included in *Lampropeltis*. It also seems to show that the scarlet kingsnake, *Lampropeltis triangulum elapsoides*, genetically is a species distinct from the rest of the milksnake subspecies and deserving of its own species, *Lampropeltis elapsoides*. For now, I'm

The scarlet kingsnake.

continuing to treat the scarlet kingsnake as a type of milksnake, but be aware that many people believe they have good evidence to call it a full species. American rat snakes, bullsnakes, and kingsnakes are very closely related and sometimes can be forced to interbreed in

Other *Lampropeltis*

Although some herpetologists argue about just how many species of kingsnakes to recognize, the following are the traditionally accepted species:

Getula group
- *Lampropeltis getula*—common kingsnake
- *Lampropeltis calligaster*—prairie kingsnake

Extenuata group
- *Lampropeltis extenuata*—short-tailed kingsnake

Triangulum group
- *Lampropeltis triangulum*—milksnake

Pyromelana group
- *Lampropeltis pyromelana*—Sonoran mountain kingsnake
- *Lampropeltis zonata*—California mountain kingsnake

Mexicana group
- *Lampropeltis mexicana*—Mexican kingsnake
- *Lampropeltis alterna*—gray-banded kingsnake
- *Lampropeltis ruthveni*—Ruthven's kingsnake
- *Lampropeltis webbi*—Webb's kingsnake

Don't pay too much attention to the groups, which are for convenience of discussion only. Recent DNA work shows that the species may be related to each other in ways different than traditionally believed by herpetologists.

captivity. In fact, some specialists want to place all the American rat snakes into the same genus as the bullsnakes, *Pituophis*. But fortunately, this controversy does not concern us here.

Species and Subspecies Challenges

Taxonomy was originally practiced more as an art than as a science, and it was (and still is) hard to get two workers to agree on all details of where and how to classify an animal. A genus is an artificial category with manmade borders, while a species is supposedly a real biological entity. The problem is that even if species are real, they are variable, and often one species varies into another, the lines between them blurring. In theory, a species is a group of similar animals that reproduce among themselves to produce similar offspring—they share a common genetic makeup. In reality, species usually are pretty much what the last or most respected worker decides is a species.

The case for subspecies is even fuzzier, as they are geographically restricted parts of a species that have generally distinctive characters but fail to hold their characters where they come into contact with other subspecies—they intergrade, in other words, to produce intermediates. Some herpetologists do not believe that subspecies are real and feel they should not be given formal scientific names. Other herpetologists believe that any somewhat recognizable segment of a species with a fairly discrete range should bear its own name. Still other workers wonder about the status of isolated populations—subspecies with ranges (geographic distribution) that do not come into contact with other subspecies. Such isolated populations are now commonly being treated as species rather than subspecies, and DNA work often backs up such changes. The isolated range of the Utah milksnake, *Lampropeltis triangulum taylori*, for instance, leads some taxonomists to suspect it should be treated as a full species.

At the moment, the namers of subspecies are in charge of milksnakes, and workers recognize as many as twenty-five subspecies within the single species of milksnake. Some of these are very distinctive in size, color, or scale counts, while others cannot be identified with certainty without knowing where the specimen was collected. Interestingly, at least a dozen of these subspecies are fairly easy to find in the terrarium and are bred in captivity on a regular basis.

The most recent revision of the milksnake, including scientific descriptions of all the subspecies, detailed maps of their ranges, and keys that help distinguish them, is a large paper by Dr. Kenneth L. Williams, "Systematics and Natural History of the American Milksnake, *Lampropeltis Triangulum*," published in 1988 by the Milwaukee Public Museum.

It is very important to note that nothing in the scientific "name game" is set in stone. Taxonomists are constantly shuffling and revising the classification system. For example, the scarlet kingsnake, *Lampropeltis triangulum elapsoides*, is sometimes considered a full species, *Lampropeltis elapsoides*. The current method of classification is a good one, and with a noble purpose, but it's far from perfect. Take the system at face value—it's good, but it's not gospel.

Overall Classification

Milksnakes belong to the phylum Chordata (vertebrates, as well as sea squirts and lancelets), subphylum Vertebrata (fish through mammals), class Reptilia (all reptiles, though whether dinosaurs and relatives should be here is controversial), the order Squamata (snakes and lizards), the suborder Serpentes (snakes), and the family Colubridae (advanced snakes).

Most snakes belong to the family Colubridae, a complex group that contains very large and very small species, a few species that glide through the air, many that burrow or swim, and a few that are venomous to humans as well as to their prey. They are the core group of snakes, neither very primitive nor very specialized, and comprise about 300 genera and perhaps 2,500 species. Although not especially common in Australia and absent from New Zealand and most of the South Pacific, colubrids are found almost everywhere else in the world.

CHAPTER 2

General Information

Befote we get to how to best care for and breed milk-snakes, let's talk a little bit about milksnakes in general. What distinguishes a milksnake from other kingsnakes? Where are the various milksnake species to be found? What are their basic patterns of behavior, and how do they reproduce? And why have they been accused of being mimics?

What Is a Milksnake?

Coming up with a real definition of for the milksnake species is difficult. Like other species of *Lampropeltis*, the milksnake has smooth, glossy scales on the body, including the sides (side scales have a ridge or keel in the species of rat snakes and gopher snakes), and the wide scale covering the vent or cloaca (anus) is single, not divided into two scales by an oblique slit as in corn snakes and rat snakes. Within the genus, the milksnake usually is distinguished by having just nineteen to twenty-one rows of scales around the body at midlength and having a narrow head not set off from the neck. A tricolored (red-black-white) pattern usually but not always is present; when the tricolored pattern is present, it usually comprises fewer than thirty white rings. The color bands usually extend around the body (although the red bands often don't make it completely around). Other tricolored, ringed kingsnakes, such as the mountain kings, generally have more than thirty white bands. There are differences in number of scales on the belly and under the tail that help define the species, as well, but most hobbyists depend on the milksnake's slender shape, small head, and color pattern to distinguish it from other species.

Range and Habitats

The milksnake is a species found exclusively in the New World. Its range starts in the north in southern Ontario, stretches west to the Rocky Mountains, and extends east to North America's Atlantic coast. It runs south through most of central and coastal Mexico, then reaches through the rest of Central America and just into South America, west of the

Milksnakes Subspecies and Ranges

For future reference, the subspecies of milksnake usually accepted are listed below, along with their known ranges.

Lampropeltis triangulum abnorma (Bocourt, 1886):
Guatemalan milksnake; Guatemala and vicinity
Lampropeltis triangulum amaura, Cope, 1861:
Louisiana milksnake; United States, Okla. and Ark. to Texas and La.—widely available
Lampropeltis triangulum andesiana, Williams, 1978: Andean milksnake; Colombia—available
Lampropeltis triangulum annulata, Kennicott, 1861: Mexican milksnake; northern Mexico to southern Texas, United States—widely available
Lampropeltis triangulum arcifera (Werner, 1903): Jalisco milksnake; western central Mexico
Lampropeltis triangulum blanchardi, Stuart, 1935: Blanchard's milksnake; Yucatán Peninsula, Mexico
Lampropeltis triangulum campbelli, Quinn, 1983: Pueblan milksnake; Puebla to Oaxaca, Mexico—widely available
Lampropeltis triangulum celaenops, Stejneger, 1903: New Mexico milksnake; United States, N.M. and adjacent Texas, into northern Mexico—available
Lampropeltis triangulum conanti, Williams, 1978: Conant's milksnake; Guerrero to Oaxaca, Mexico
Lampropeltis triangulum dixoni, Quinn, 1983: Dixon's milksnake; San Luis Potosi to Guanajuato, Mexico
Lampropeltis triangulum elapsoides (Holbrook, 1838): scarlet kingsnake; United States, Va. to Fla., Tenn., and Miss.— widely available; often considered a full species because range overlaps with that of eastern milksnake in several areas without intergrading

Andes Mountains, in Colombia, Ecuador, and northern Venezuela. Nine subspecies are found only or almost only within the United States and Canada and thirteen in Mexico (two of which, *annulata* and *celaenops*, are shared with the

Lampropeltis triangulum gaigeae, Dunn, 1937: black milksnake; Costa Rica and Panama—available

Lampropeltis triangulum gentilis (Baird and Girard, 1853): Central Plains milksnake; United States, Neb. and Colo. to Texas—available

Lampropeltis triangulum hondurensis, Williams, 1978: Hon-duran milksnake; Honduras to Costa Rica— widely available

Lampropeltis triangulum micropholis, Cope, 1860: Ecuadoran milksnake; Costa Rica to Ecuador—available

Lampropeltis triangulum multistriata, Kennicott, 1860: pale milksnake; United States, N.D. and Mont. to Neb.—available

Lampropeltis triangulum nelsoni, Blanchard, 1920: Nelson's milksnake; southwestern Mexico—widely available

Lampropeltis triangulum oligozona (Bocourt, 1886): Pacific Central American milksnake; Oaxaca and Chiapas, Mexico, to Guatemala

Lampropeltis triangulum polyzona (Cope, 1861): Atlantic Central American milksnake; Veracruz, Mexico, to Belize

Lampropeltis triangulum sinaloae, Williams, 1978: Sinaloan milksnake; Sonora to Sinaloa, Mexico—widely available

Lampropeltis triangulum smithi, Williams, 1978: Smith's milksnake; northern central Mexico

Lampropeltis triangulum stuarti, Williams, 1978: Stuart's milksnake; El Salvador to Costa Rica—available

Lampropeltis triangulum syspila (Cope, 1888): red milksnake; United States, S.D. to Okla. and Miss.—widely available

Lampropeltis triangulum taylori, Tanner and Loomis, 1957: Utah milksnake; United States, Colo. to Utah and Ariz.

Lampropeltis triangulum triangulum (Lacépède, 1788): eastern milksnake; southeastern Canada and the United States, Minn. to Mass., south to Ky.—widely available

The red milksnake can typically be found between South Dakota and Mississippi.

United States); only two subspecies (*andesiana and micropholis*) enter northwestern South America west of the Andes Mountains. This gives the milksnake one of the largest, if not the largest, range of any American snake and perhaps the largest of any snake in the world.

Not surprisingly, given their wide geographic range, milksnakes can be found in a wide variety of environmental niches. They are found in forested mountains, near lakes, in forests ranging from pine to oaks, in rolling prairies, in parched deserts, in swamps, and in just about everything in between. They are capable climbers and swimmers but prefer to spend the bulk of their time under logs, rocks, and other debris on the surface of the soil. Some forms found in wet habitats often are dug from stumps in standing water. Milksnakes are hardy and highly adaptable, which has helped make them good pets in the terrarium.

Habits

As a general rule, milksnakes are nocturnal, coming out of hiding around dusk and disappearing by the early morning hours. Like most other reptiles, they are opportunistic, following their impulses and the dictates of their circumstances. If the temperature grows too high, they will seek shelter until the cooler evening or night hours. If they are hungry enough, however, they'll hunt for food at any time. Seasonally, they tend to breed in the spring, lay their eggs in the early summer, hatch their young by September, "relax and unwind" into the fall, and go dormant in the winter. (In warmer climes, where they won't experience a full hibernation or brumation period, they go through a period of greatly reduced activity called *estivation*.) These generalities, however, don't apply to all of the subspecies; those of tropical uplands, for instance, obviously do not recognize the same seasonal patterns as milksnakes from New England.

For the most part, milksnakes are calm, gentle, and peaceful creatures, only attacking when hungry or threatened. The smaller subspecies tend to feed on lizards when young, as do babies of most species, while most larger adults feed on rodents and nestling birds. The prey is grasped in the flexible jaws using their dozens of teeth and usually then constricted until breathing stops. They commonly eat prey measuring about one and a half times the size of their own heads.

Reproduction

There are few external distinctions between the sexes in milksnakes. Males do tend to have thicker, longer tail bases than females do to house the deeply forked penis, split into two distinct branches (the hemipenes), typical of snakes

The time of year in which *triangulum* mates varies with locality (as with all reptile species), but speaking generally, they do so from March to May and lay their eggs from May to July. The eggs hatch between July and September. Because different subspecies of milksnake vary in length from just 2 feet to more than 5 feet, there can be quite a range in clutch size. The number of eggs in a clutch varies tremendously—anywhere from two or three to twenty-four, with smaller females generally laying fewer eggs than larger females do.

Hatchling milks measure around 5 to 10 inches in length;

the smallest are not as thick as an ordinary pencil. They often look gangly and vulnerable, especially with their disproportionately large heads, which seem even larger because of their bulging eyes. Some subspecies are not as brightly colored as babies as they will be in adulthood (white bands turning yellow), whereas others are stunning from the moment they emerge from their eggs. A few tropical forms tend to turn deep brown to black when fully grown.

Mimicry

The milksnake belongs to a relatively large group of tricolored snakes that are ringed, saddled, or blotched with black and red on a whitish to yellow background. For about a century, these snakes have generally been said to be copying the distinctive color patterns of similarly colored local venomous snakes and thus gaining protection from predators. The idea is that birds and mammals that feed on snakes learn that bites from brightly colored venomous snakes are painful and disabling, and after their first attack on such a venomous snake, these animals

Harmless tricolored snakes are thought by some to mimic the colors and patterns of venemous snakes, such as this coral snake.

Mimicry: A Trick of the Mind?

The whole idea of mimicry may just be coincidence, with the human mind looking to find relationships that are not real. Our primate brain likes to group things and sometimes makes very strange groupings (from a scientific sense), such as snakes and earthworms.

learn to avoid those snakes and any other snakes with similar colors and patterns. Snakes that are harmless or nearly so and copy the tricolored pattern of local venomous snakes are often called mimics. Many other groups of animals are involved in mimicry; tasty (to predators) viceroy butterflies, for instance, mimic the coloring of unappetizing monarch butterflies.

The American tropics are filled with harmless tricolored snakes in a variety of unrelated genera, but in North America the classic example of venomous snake mimicry has been the milksnake's resemblance to the southern U.S. species of coral snakes, *Micrurus fulvius* and *M. tener*. If a subspecies such as *L. t. elapsoides* (*elapsoides* actually means "like a coral snake") is compared with the eastern coral snake, *Micrurus fulvius*, the similarities are indeed amazing. The two snakes, though not at all related (they belong to different families), both have small heads and are slender, glossy, and brightly ringed with red, black, and yellow. The eastern coral snake ranges from eastern Louisiana to southern North Carolina, entirely within the range of the scarlet kingsnake. Both are nocturnal burrowing snakes that feed mostly on smaller snakes and lizards. The pattern of ring colors is different: red touches yellow in the coral snake, red touches black in the kingsnake—thus the old saying "Red touching yellow, bad for a fellow; red touching black, good for Jack" often used to separate milksnakes from coral snakes.

Once you get out of the range of the eastern coral snake, however, you begin to have problems with the mimicry theory.

The Texas coral snake, *Micrurus tener*, is found from central Louisiana to western Texas (and then into Mexico) but only barely north into Oklahoma and Arkansas. This puts it out of the range of most of the tricolored subspecies of milksnakes found in the Great Plains and Ohio Valley, so what would those subspecies be mimicking? There is no coral snake in the range of such subspecies of *L. t. gentilis*, *L. t. syspila*, and *L. t. taylori*. There also is no evidence that the range of the coral snakes was significantly more northern before the last ice age, when most of the U.S. subspecies of milksnake probably evolved.

The problems with the theory of coral snake mimicry become even larger in Mexico, where there are over a dozen species of coral snakes, many with patterns much like the Texas coral snake but others lacking red or not so obviously ringed. The Mexican milksnake subspecies don't show any special resemblance to the types of coral snakes found in their range—they tend to just have a variation of the usual red-black-white rings of the more-northerly milksnakes.

The western coral snake, *Micruroides euryxanthus*, is basically a Mexican species that ranges north into central Arizona and adjacent New Mexico. It looks much like a small, delicate version of the Texas coral snake with nearly equally wide color rings and a black head. It actually bears little resemblance to the local tricolored kingsnakes, both *Lampropeltis triangulum* and *L. pyromelana*. The other brightly ringed kingsnake, the California mountain kingsnake, *L. zonata*, has always been well outside the range of any coral snake. One pattern of the gray-banded kingsnake, *L. alterna*, seems to be a mimic of the local pattern of a small rattlesnake.

This annoying absence of consistency between the occurrence of ringed venomous snakes (the models) and similarly ringed harmless snakes (the mimics) has brought many scientists to believe that snakes such as the milksnake really do not mimic the coral snakes but instead draw on the same factors that make bird and mammal predators avoid coral snakes to begin with—bright colors in an easy to recognize pattern. The snakes are active mostly at night, when the actual colors are not easy to distinguish but the pattern of dark and light can be seen.

CHAPTER 3

Before You Buy

Buying a milksnake is a long-term commitment that deserves some thought. Although milks are great pets, they really aren't for everyone. Among the factors you must consider are the comfort of other family members with snakes; the cost of housing, feeding, and caring for your snake; the legalities of owning a particular species of snake; and possible allergies and other medical concerns for household members.

Family Involvement

You may want to buy or collect a milksnake, but think for a moment about how the rest of your family might react. Many people simply do not like snakes; in fact, a dislike or even fear of snakes is probably more common than a love of snakes. Never purchase a milksnake or any other snake without making sure that you will not cause turmoil in your home. Check that everyone in the home, including regular visitors, will not mind sharing their space with a snake, even a harmless, colorful little snake.

If you find someone you love is fearful of any snake, consider convincing them that the snake will be securely housed in a closed part of the home in a cage that you can lock. Although locking cages are not necessary for milksnakes, sometimes just the presence of a lock on the snake cage can give a person a bit of extra confidence and clear the way to bringing your snake into the home. If that fails, then consider establishing your snake—and the other snakes that are sure to follow—in a separate room or even building. The odds are good anyway that after you succeed with one milksnake you probably will want more and then will want to branch out into other types of snakes. Maybe a snake room is a good idea from the beginning if you can afford it. Think of what you can do with a separate cooling and heating system!

Costs

Milksnakes are simple snakes to keep and need only minimal housing for success, but there are still costs involved in keeping them. So when considering buying a snake, ask yourself whether you can afford to house and feed one properly. Before you go into a shop to buy a milksnake, you should already have its terrarium set up and waiting for it. You won't be able to keep that snake in a paper bag, remember. This means that before the cost of the snake comes the cost of a terrarium tank, a cover, an undertank heater, and a basking light, plus substrate and "furniture" (water and food bowls, hide boxes, and other cover). These items usually cost as much as or even several times more than the snake itself does.

Don't count on reducing snake-food costs by catching your own mice. House mice carry a variety of diseases from tapeworms to serious bacterial and viral infections that can be passed not only to the snake but also to you and your family. (That's why you try to get rid of house mice to begin with!) Milksnakes also need a variety of sizes of mice, from newly born pinkys to adults, depending on the age and subspecies of the snake. These have to be purchased, often a dozen or more at a time, from dealers in food rodents. Milksnakes don't have to eat every week, but they do need regular feedings, and a single adult milksnake can easily go through 50 to 100 mice a year. Can you afford to keep your snake in mice?

In calculating expenses, don't forget the cost of electricity and/or gas for heating and cooling your snake area. An undertank heater and basking light may be running most of the day for at least eight months a year. In some cases, you may have to cool the snake during the warmest days of summer or during the overwintering period necessary for fertile eggs. Energy is no longer cheap and really has to be considered today in the cost of a snake.

Legalities

The legality of selling milksnakes in pet shops and collecting them from nature varies from place to place, so be sure to check with your local environmental agency beforehand.

Mouse Concerns

Will the other people in your home be willing to share their space with rodents?

In the terrarium, milksnakes feed almost exclusively on mice of different ages, and you will have to refrigerate the ones you buy to feed your snakes. Your refrigerator or freezer probably will always have a dozen or so mice stored in it. How will the rest of your family react to mice in the freezer? Although the mice have been captive-bred under excellent conditions and are clean, they are still rodents, and many people cannot stand the thought of their food in the same refrigerator or freezer as a dead mouse. Colonies of living mice are even worse because they smell and produce lots of waste. Where will you keep your living or dead mice when you buy your milksnake?

Fuzzies kept in a separate habitat for future feeding.

No matter what kind of milksnake you buy, make sure you purchase it lawfully. A little research is really worth the effort when you look at the consequences of buying or owning snakes illegally.

Such information can be found on the Web and is therefore readily available. Commonly, a shop cannot sell a subspecies that is native to the state where the shop is located. Some forms of milksnake are protected in states where they are uncommon or rare, states that may be at the edges of the milksnake species' range. In a few cities, all snake sales may be prohibited. Abide by local regulations—if you try to go around the laws, you are sure to be caught, fined, and have your snake confiscated and perhaps destroyed.

Laws change in an unpredictable fashion, so it is not possible to give any details here. However, as a general rule, you cannot be sure that a snake is legal just because you can buy one at a local reptile show or even from a pet shop. Dealers may not always know exactly what is legal and what is not in your particular town or city. What is legal to sell and own in Jackson, Mississippi, may be illegal in Atlanta, Georgia. Additionally, most states today have methods for restricting or at least keeping track of snake ownership. Some officials require that you fill out and submit a permit application for each snake you purchase or collect, including snakes as diverse as rattlesnakes and milksnakes. In many states, you must purchase a yearly hunting or fishing license to enable you not only to collect snakes legally in the state but also to possess them; there may even be possession limits—generally allowing just one or two specimens of a species. There may be a strong emphasis in local laws on restricting or prohibiting ownership of not only endangered or threatened species and subspecies but also any species (not just subspecies) native to that state. To possess a species native to the state, you may have to PIT tag your snake (see "Pit Tags" in chapter 11, Diseases and Disorders) at additional cost and promise you will not breed it.

Because regulations vary so greatly, you must try to find out all local—your state, county, and town—regulations as they apply to keeping snakes, including milksnakes. We hobbyists know that milks are small, harmless, adorable snakes, but your local councilperson or legislator may disagree. Check before you find yourself on the wrong side of the law.

Allergies and Medical Concerns

Snakes generally are considered to be allergen-free pets, but that may not be completely accurate. Milksnakes and other snakes produce airborne detritus in the form of fragments of shed skin that could leave their terrarium and cause some allergic reactions in you or family members. In addition, the mice that you feed your milksnake are hairy, and that hair can cause allergic reactions in sensitive persons.

Like other animals (including humans), snakes have a variety of bacteria in their intestines that help in digestion. When these bacteria escape alive and contaminate the substrate, they can be transferred to humans and cause intestinal upset such as salmonella and, rarely, more serious problems. Keeping your snake terrarium clean and feeding only quality mice will virtually eliminate the salmonella problem, but it always exists. Although salmonella is a mild disease in most people, it can very rarely cause death in babies, seniors, and immune-compromised persons. This danger must be considered before bringing a snake into the home.

CHAPTER 4

Selecting and Purchasing Your Milksnake

You've decided that you want to keep a milksnake of some type. Now how do you go about finding a nice, colorful specimen in your price range? Do you go to a pet shop, or would it be better to contact a breeder? How do you access a specific milksnake to determine whether it is a good specimen or not? Should you—and can you legally—just collect a snake from the wild instead of purchasing one? Is that even a good idea? This chapter will help you answer those questions.

Determining the Kind

Before you buy a snake, you need to decide which "model" of milksnake you want. What species most appeals to you—and is legal to own in your area? Do you want a relatively inexpensive North American form or a more colorful and more expensive tropical subspecies?

Baby milksnakes, such as these "Jurassic" milksnakes, can be a lot of fun to care for, but if your goal is to breed, you may want to purchase adult snakes so that you don't have to wait the requisite two to three years for the babies to mature.

Do you want a newborn, or do you want an adult? Are you hoping to breed it some day, or do you just want a little friend? Maintaining a baby milksnake can be a treat. Similar to the newborns of most other animals, baby milksnakes are as cute as can be (even if they do show a little temper every now and then). If you give them the proper care and attention, they will thrive in captivity and grow into marvelous companions. However, as we will see, some (the Louisiana milksnake and the scarlet kingsnake, for example) are so tiny that you might have considerable trouble getting food for them. Immature milksnakes also have a higher mortality rate than older specimens. (You should expect an average milksnake to live at least twelve years in the terrarium.)

Regardless, you should be sensitive to what you really want—if your ultimate goal is to breed milksnakes, remember that it will take about two or three years for a newborn to reach sexual maturity. If you want to buy adults, however, then you have to be prepared to furnish them with plenty of living space. Milksnakes, while small in the general snake spectrum, are still relatively large creatures. They certainly won't be happy in a small aquarium tank turned into a terrarium. In terms of owning a milksnake, one of the main questions becomes, are you ready and willing to give it the space it will need to be truly content?

Determining Where to Buy

Now that you have an idea of what species and age of milksnake you want, you need to decide on the best place to find it. Do you go to a pet shop or a breeder? Would you rather see the snake in person or will looking at images on the Web be enough?

Pet Shops

Most people head to a pet shop to obtain new snake specimens. The majority of pet shops offer convenience, good service, and a varied selection of livestock. In addition, due to the rise in popularity of the herpetological hobby, many shops now offer at least a few reptiles and amphibians, including

The red milksnake is widely available, affordable, and great for beginning herpers.

the larger and more common milksnakes—especially Hondurans, Sinaloans, Mexicans, and reds.

Spend a little time inspecting each pet store you visit before buying anything. If you're going to buy an animal from a shop, it's important that you like the shop. Cleanliness is, of course, a huge consideration. Be fair and understand that pet shops naturally harbor a large number of animals, so they won't exactly be as clean as operating rooms. With that in mind, however, you should still be comfortable with what you see, hear, smell, and touch. If the place is really filthy, go to a different store.

Returns

Don't hesitate to ask whether the store has any kind of return policy. Buying an animal isn't like buying a car—no one's going to give you a five-year warranty. Most shops, however, will at least guarantee the health of the animal for a period long enough to allow you to have it examined by a veterinarian. Commonly, a store will accept a return for up to a week; sometimes longer periods are specified by state laws. If the store is reluctant to offer any type of guarantee, you might want to go somewhere else.

More and more herp hobbyists are looking to commercial and hobby breeders for pets. Breeders offer a number of advantages over pet shops. Perhaps the most obvious is that the buyer knows the animal from a breeder has been captive-bred, which means it has never spent a day in the wild. That means the odds of the animal's harboring any kind of bacteria or parasites normally found in wild specimens is very low. In addition, and again because the snake has never been in the wild, it will already be well accustomed to life in captivity. That may sound a bit cruel, but the reality is that the animal doesn't know what it never had, so the chances of its being restless and stressed because of the domestic environment are greatly reduced. Another positive is that when you buy an animal you know was hatched and raised in captivity, it means one fewer animal has been taken from the wild.

Mail Order and the Internet. These days, you shouldn't have a hard time finding a reliable and experienced breeder. There was a time when you had to search high and low to find a breeder of milksnakes, but thanks to the great strides made in herpetoculture in the 1990s, and again thanks to the conveniences afforded us via the Internet and mail order, there are more people breeding reptiles than ever before—and they're easier to locate, too. Additionally, let's not forget that milksnakes are among the most commonly bred snake species.

Reptile magazines and the newsletters of regional herpetological societies usually have many ads by breeders of milksnakes, including a variety of subspecies and color varieties. If that doesn't work for you, then try the Web. Open your browser, go to a search engine, and type in obvious search words such as "milksnake breeder" or "Lampropeltis triangulum." Chances are that you'll end up with more online price lists than you ever imagined. With that many lists, you're truly in a buyer's market, and that means you'll have choices. Sooner or later you'll find the breeder—and thereby the specimen—that is right for you, not to mention the best specimen. There's never been a better time to be a milksnake enthusiast.

Two downsides to shopping on the Web and by mail order are that many people don't like doing business with strangers, and they don't like buying animals without seeing them first. This is perfectly understandable; there's nothing wrong with wanting to protect yourself from an unscrupulous seller.

Live Herp Shows. Anyone interested in purchasing a milksnake should make a point of attending a live herp show (which is essentially a breeders' convention or expo). There are so many of these now that listing them all would fill pages. You'll find a huge selection of creatures from all walks of the herp kingdom (but be careful—you may find your enthusiasm divided between milksnakes and something else new and fascinating). Chances are that quite a few of the vendors will have milksnakes for sale. You can inspect them and make your purchase right on the spot. Don't worry about getting shafted by some shady, shifty, fast-buck operator—99 percent of the sellers at these shows are friendly with everyone in the herp community, from the people running the show to dozens of other buyers. Remember, these are people trying to run a successful business, so they're not going to blow their reputation on a minor sale; the idea is to develop a list of repeat customers. Don't be afraid to ask around and gather up some references. The herp world still isn't so big that reputations just vanish in the mix. It's a bit like small town America—everybody knows everybody. Finding a reputable dealer won't be a problem.

What to Avoid

Whenever you purchase a milksnake in person, you have to spend a few minutes checking the snake for potential problems. Look around its eyes to make sure they're clear. Is there any runniness from the nostrils? How does the skin look? Is it dull and dirty, or taut and bright? Does the animal act lively when you touch it, or is it listless and lethargic? Are there any signs of serious scarring, new wounds, or possible broken bones (especially in the back and the jaws)? You're probably not a trained vet who can spot a sick animal on first sight, but common sense should be enough to tell you whether or not the animal you're examin-

Shipping

One major disadvantage of purchasing a milksnake over the Web or through a mail-order ad is that you will have to have it shipped to you. This is not a simple process, as the postal service and most major mail carrier companies do not allow you to ship snakes. This means that if you buy a snake from a distant breeder, either you have to travel to the breeder to pick it up or you will need to pay for air freight shipping and pick up the snake at the closest airport. Air freight is expensive and not available during all seasons or in all parts of the country. Commonly, the cost of air freight (not to mention the inconvenience) is half or more the cost of the snake itself. Before you agree to buy a milksnake over the Internet or by mail, be sure that you understand exactly how much shipping will cost you and just how easy or difficult it will be to pick it up. This is one of the reasons that potential buyers of milksnakes and other snakes look for reptile shows.

ing is in satisfactory health. However, once you have the snake, it never hurts to spend a bit of money and have any new purchase examined by a veterinarian who is familiar with snakes. The vet expense may equal the cost of the snake, but at least you can be sure that there are no obvious problems.

Shedding problems are often encountered with milk-snakes that are kept in very dry conditions, as in a pet-shop terrarium. Snakes molt their skin on a fairly regular basis (usually at least twice a year in older adults, perhaps every six to ten weeks in growing young) so they can grow. The skin comes off as a single piece (or nearly so), inverted from the snout back to the tail like a sock pulled off your foot from the top down. If the snake has mites or is kept too dry, however, the molt can be patchy, the skin breaking into many small pieces. Some of these can adhere to the new skin and cause problems, so keep an eye out for this when shopping.

A healthy snake sheds its skin in a single piece, not in flakes.

Collecting from the Wild

Taking milksnakes and other snakes from the wild is a controversial topic, and both sides of the issue have good arguments.

In Blue

About three to five days before a milksnake sheds, its eyes turn blue and opaque. During this time, you should make a water bath available and provide a rough surface to let the snake break the skin on the snout to start the shed. The normal color usually returns about two days before the shed itself. The change in color is due to fluid accumulating between the old and new skins. Note: Never help a snake molt—you will cause more problems than solutions.

Those who argue against collecting start with the fact that these creatures have spent their entire lives in the same areas, becoming familiar with every inch of soil, every drop of water, every tree, and every bush. When you take them away from that, they can become frightened, confused, and highly stressed. Most wild-caught animals make bad captives, and milksnakes are no exception. They can be unwilling to eat once they've been taken from their natural surroundings, and the rate at which these snakes decline is heartbreaking. If this is the case, you're not keeping an enjoyable pet at this point; you're just killing it slowly.

Another argument against collecting involves medical problems. How do you know, for example, that the milksnake you just brought home doesn't have a well-developed case of mouth rot or a mite infestation? You would not want to find out only after the problem has spread to the rest of the animals in your collection. So, if you do collect a specimen, you must exercise proper caution. Just as you would when adding a new captive-bred snake to your collection, be sure to quarantine the newly harvested snake and take it to a veterinarian for a full exam as soon as possible.

The Honduran milksnake in its natural environment.

In addition, don't forget that, as stated above, there could be legal repercussions for collecting a wild specimen. In many places, taking animals from the wild is a crime punishable by heavy fines, jail time, or both. Collect from private property without written permission and you could end up with charges of trespassing. Know the local laws before even thinking about harvesting a wild snake.

In many states, it is possible to obtain permits to collect a few reptiles as pets or to collect them legally if you already have a hunting or fishing license. Some people believe that as long as you are not selling the animals and take very few specimens (and few milksnakes are so abundant that they are likely to be collected in quantity), you are having little impact on the snakes in the wild. According to these hobbyists, destruction of habitat—not the occasional harvesting of specimens—is the true killer of snake populations.

Many wild-caught milksnakes adjust well to captivity.

Many hobbyists believe that collecting from the wild should not be simply cast aside but should not be done haphazardly either. Remember that all captive-bred snakes came from what was once wild-caught stock. In some cases, it is likely that there are now more captive-bred members of a subspecies than there are members living in the wild. If a milksnake is known to be uncommon or to have a very small range, then obviously you should not collect one from the wild—it is probably available as captive-bred anyway. Overall, collectors believe that collecting carefully and only under circumstances that will not hurt a milksnake's population can be a viable alternative to purchasing specimen.

Juvenile specimens often adapt much more readily to captive conditions and can thrive in a terrarium. Many wild-caught milksnakes feed well in captivity after a period of adjustment, though very young specimens are, as usual, often a problem. Given proper terrarium conditions and gentle handling, many wild milksnakes turn into great pets—as good as any captive-bred snake. In addition, many hobbyists who live in areas where milksnakes are common and are often found on roads during the spring and autumn believe that collecting such LOR (live on road) specimens actually saves them from death under the wheels of a car.

Perhaps one of the best compromises in the argument between whether or not to collect snakes is to photograph milksnakes in nature instead. Many people enjoy the hunt for a specimen but don't really want to take it home. The trophy can be a good photo instead. Because of today's digital cameras, good photography is easier than ever, and the images can even be transmitted to friends over the Internet.

CHAPTER 5

Housing and Maintenance

Correctly housing a milksnake isn't all that difficult. It requires a fair amount of space and sometimes a bit of work on the part of the keeper, but don't let this discourage you. When properly executed, providing your milksnakes with a nice place to live can be a fun, educational, and exhilarating experience. Just choosing the type of housing is only the beginning, however. You must also find out what the heat and humidity requirements are for your particular species and purchase the right equipment to meet those requirements. Proper substrates, lighting, water bowls, and other furnishings (such as hide boxes) are essential, as well. Keeping everything clean—including your snake—is as important as providing proper housing.

Types of Housing

The majority of reptile and amphibian pets are kept in glass aquaria (fish tanks). Aquaria offer a great measure of security (as long as a tight-fitting top is included, of course), the opportunity to easily view your pets, and a practical and efficient method of cleaning (simply wash the glass with mild soap and water, sometimes aided with vinegar). There are some drawbacks to these aquaria, however, so some hobbyists prefer buying other types of enclosures or even building their own.

Glass Aquaria

Aquaria are perfectly suitable for milksnakes. They come in a wide range of shapes and sizes, so even larger milksnakes will be comfortable. They are readily available at most pet shops at reasonable prices, and if you can't find a model to your liking,

A glass aquarium made suitable for a snake.

you can either try another shop or order the right one. As for the best size, the larger the better, though in reality a single milksnake needs little space. As long as you've provided an aquarium large enough for your snake to stretch out completely, you'll be OK. Remember that no more than two adult milksnakes should ever occupy the same enclosure. It's simply cruel to stuff too many animals into one tank. Whatever you do, don't keep milksnakes of greatly different sizes together— if hungry enough, milksnakes (like the other species of the genus *Lampropeltis*) will eat other snakes, including those of their own species. You may come home one day to find one very fat snake instead of two slim ones.

Other Types of Terraria

Aquaria are the most readily available type of terrarium, but they certainly are not the only satisfactory type of unit—or, necessarily, the best. Not all hobbyists like glass aquaria, which tend to be heavy and to hold in more humidity than might be good for the snake. Through dealers, you can find a variety of other types of snake terraria, ranging from large fiberglass shells with sliding glass doors to units designed to hold a dozen or

Security

Here's an important note on security: always make sure your snake's terrarium has a snug-fitting top with security clips to hold it down. Such clips can be found at most pet shops that stock herp-related items. Remember that snakes are by nature skilled escape artists, able to make the most of even the tiniest opportunities. They sit around all day with very little to do, and, like inmates of a prison, will inspect every millimeter of their enclosure for signs of weakness. Again, always make sure the top is on tight, and the security clips are firmly in place.

more plastic trays for snakes being used in breeding programs. Look on the Internet and check the ads in reptile magazines to get an idea of some of the other designs available.

Home-Built Enclosures

Some keepers choose to build custom enclosures for their pets. The advantages here are obvious—you can make the enclosure as large as you want, and you can include loads of bells and whistles.

Wood is the most common raw material. Please note, however, that ordinary wood does not respond well to repeated cleanings, wood tends to accrue fungus quickly when wet, and has crevices that are excellent homes for mites. Many home-improvement stores are now offering lengths of wood precovered by snake-friendly materials such as laminate. I strongly suggest that any would-be terrarium builders use this kind of product not only for health reasons but also because it is often precut in convenient lengths and is easy to cut further to exact specifications.

Again, make sure the enclosure you build can be secured, and take your time with the predesign work. Don't just hurriedly nail a box together and hope for the best. Building a terrarium can be a very exciting project! Plan it out carefully, factoring in your viewing pleasure, the multitude of practical considerations, and the comfort of your pet(s). A smartly conceived enclosure can provide both you and your pets with years of pleasure and enjoyment.

Climatic Requirements

Because they are cold-blooded creatures from tropical to temperate climes, milksnakes will naturally need special consideration for their heat and humidity. During the day, the ambient temperature in their enclosure should be anywhere from 75 to 80 degrees Fahrenheit, with about a 4-degree drop during the night. As for humidity, you need to know where your particular specimen came from and replicate the amount of humidity from that environment. Those from the southern end of the range (Central America and northwestern South America) will obviously need more humidity than those from the northern end (the northeastern United States, for example). You'll need to do a little homework here, but not too much. Most milksnakes do well at 60 to 70 percent relative humidity much of the year.

Humidity

You can provide humidity very easily by including a small bowl with a wet sponge in your snake's enclosure. Situate the bowl directly on or under the heating device. The heat will

Misting

Many hobbyists find it convenient to increase the humidity in the terrarium by misting each day. An inexpensive plastic misting bottle sold for use with plants works well, but a better quality nursery mister made of metal will last longer and produce a finer mist that is more effective. Additionally, there are misting machines of various types available from pet shops to increase the humidity to higher levels, but they really aren't necessary for milksnakes.

draw the moisture from the sponge and in turn make the atmosphere more humid. You should obtain a hygrometer so you can accurately monitor and measure the amount of humidity. You can then control it through how wet you make the sponge each time you remoisten it. Of course, misting the terrarium once or twice a day can also provide the correct level of humidity, and much more easily.

Make sure the enclosure is properly ventilated. Too much air movement will allow most of the humidity to escape, but too little will cause the air to quickly stagnate, creating a very unhealthy environment for your captives and the basis for bacterial growth. This is one disadvantage of a glass aquarium for a terrarium—it is almost impossible to properly ventilate it. Many other terrarium designs have screened panels toward the bottom of one side to allow more air flow.

Heating

You have a large variety of heating apparatuses to choose from these days—everything from lamps to pads to "hot rocks." All but hot rocks are suitable for milksnakes. But the best options, at least in my opinion, are those that provide the snakes with a temperature gradient. For example, a heating pad placed under the terrarium at one end will not greatly change the temperature at the opposite end, thus allowing the snakes to enjoy whatever

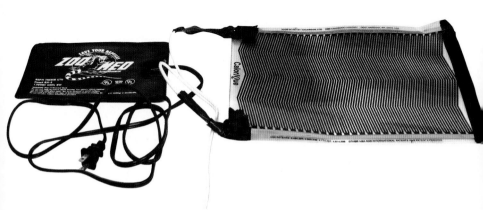

An undertank heating pad.

Nighttime

Here's a good idea—turn off any heating devices after dark (or at least turn them down, if that's possible). Even in the warmest regions on Earth, it's normal for the temperature to decrease after the sun goes down (this is especially important with desert snakes). The change in temperature should be the same in captivity. If you still fear your animals will get cold, include a second heating device (something small and relatively weak) that they can use during the night. The main idea with the provision of heat, of course, is to replicate whatever temperature cycles exist in a specimen's native habitat. A timer makes it easy to provide slightly different day and night temperature regimens.

temperature their wishes dictate. This is a familiar type of temperature gradient, with one end of the terrarium at perhaps 70 degrees Fahrenheit and the other at 80 or 85 degrees Fahrenheit.

Most keepers today probably use a combination of a small undertank heating pad (one that glues onto the bottom of the terrarium, especially if it is a glass aquarium) and an incandescent light above the terrarium. In addition, the room where the snake is kept must be warm much of the year; the temperature must not being allowed to drop much below 70 degrees Fahrenheit. Some hobbyists use quartz or oil-filled heaters during the winter to maintain a moderately warm room temperature to make heating a terrarium easier and cheaper.

Be absolutely certain that no heating device provides too much heat. For example, no milksnake is going to want to sit under a lamp that's warming a certain spot to 125 degrees Fahrenheit. Make sure, as well, that your heating device isn't warming the entire enclosure. When that happens, more often than not you'll find your snake lying in its water bowl in a desperate attempt to cool off. This is one of the main drawbacks of hot rock heaters—they can develop very warm areas that can literally cook a snake, which cannot detect or react to such warm spots. (Snakes tend to sense heat mostly on their backs and are relatively insensitive to heat coming from below.)

Of course, you will need at least one—preferably two—thermometers in the terrarium so you know how the temperature is faring. Small electronic thermometers are easy to find now and are inexpensive. Some measure the temperature not only around the basic unit but also at a remote sensor that can be placed exactly where you want to measure the temperature, such as under a basking light. Additionally, many electronic thermometer units include a fairly accurate hygrometer, which measures relative humidity in the terrarium.

Other Equipment and Furnishings

In addition to providing for your snake's heat and humidity requirements, you need to furnish your enclosure with the proper substrate, lighting, water bowls, hiding places, plants, and branches for climbing.

Substrates

A substrate is the material that covers the floor of an enclosure—the bedding or litter. In herpetoculture, there are virtually

This enclosure uses wood shavings for bedding, which is typical of milksnake terraria.

End Rolls

Often you can get unprinted newspaper end rolls (the unused paper at the end of a printing roll of paper) at the offices of a local newspaper that still prints its weekly shoppers and the like locally. Be sure to get coarse, uncoated newspaper; coated newspaper such as is used to print color or for Sunday supplements is not as absorbent as plain newspaper.

dozens of types of substrates. Snake terraria are often bedded with newspaper, which is cheap and easy to replace but doesn't look very good. Newspaper is often used when large numbers of milksnakes are kept, as for a breeding program. Paper toweling is a step up, but it also does not look very natural.

Most hobbyists today probably use some type of wood shavings for a substrate. Pine shavings are good and relatively inexpensive. Aspen shavings are better, although they cost more. Some keepers like different types of bark mulch, which may hold more water and keep the relative humidity higher. Wood seems to be the way to go today, though there are some herpers who like unusual materials such as processed corncobs or treated coconut fibers. In the typical terrarium, a 2-inch layer of shavings is put down over the floor and changed every week to every month, depending on conditions. The shavings absorb urine and feces to some extent and look good with just daily "touchups" and spot cleanings. Throw away or burn old shavings—don't try to clean and recycle them.

Never use cedar shavings in a snake terrarium—cedar gives off oils that, in the confines of a terrarium, may cause liver and other internal problems in a captive snake.

Years ago keepers used sand, rocks, and potting soil for substrates, and really there is no reason why these cannot be used if you wish. All are heavy and can be difficult to clean, but to some keepers, they look much more natural than wood shavings. Often, as a compromise, a portion of the floor of the

A milksnake basking in the light from an incandescent light bulb.

terrarium can be bedded in a mixture of soil, vermiculite, and peat moss that looks very natural and can serve as a good place for plants.

Proper Lighting

Milksnakes, which are night active, don't really need to bask in full-spectrum lighting to flourish as turtles and lizards do. A full-spectrum light tries to mimic the wavelengths of sunlight that are most efficient at converting vitamin precursors to vitamin D3, which controls the metabolism and deposition of calcium. Basking reptiles need this type of lighting to ensure good health, but milksnakes are largely nocturnal, and many do not bask on a regular schedule. Full-spectrum bulbs and their fixtures can be expensive, so it's just as well that milksnakes can live without them.

Many longtime keepers and breeders of milksnakes insist that such lighting makes their pets healthier and happier, adds as much as five years to their lives, and doubles the size of a female's egg clutch. However, there is no really solid evidence to back up these claims.

Recent experiments with nocturnal lizards have shown that even these nighttime animals bask for brief intervals as the sun goes down or rises. Just fifteen minutes of exposure to weak sunlight allows the lizard to make enough vitamin D to control its calcium levels. The same is probably true of nocturnal snakes, which are often seen to become active either just before the sun goes down completely or to remain active until just after the sun rises.

Milksnakes do need lighting, of course, to help set their body's cycles. Most hobbyists use a 25- to 50-watt incandescent bulb in a conical reflector aimed at a rock or branch where the snakes might like to bask occasionally. Some milksnakes seldom bask, while others like to lie in a warm spot for an hour or two a day. This type of light also helps heat the terrarium.

No matter what type of lighting you decide to use, all you need to do with it is suspend it over the enclosure. No light bulb, incandescent or fluorescent, should ever be placed inside the terrarium—this is sure to lead to burns, as snakes tend to coil around such lights. Even if you enclose the lights in shields, the shields will get hot and cause burns. Lights—especially incandescent ones—are typically placed on top of the screen lid or suspended a foot or so above the terrarium, out of the snake's reach.

You should set up the light with a timer and set the timer so the light is on for about eight hours a day. It is also perfectly acceptable to place the snake's terrarium near a window and let the snake be exposed to natural day and night cycles. Just be careful that direct sunlight does not heat the cage to unhealthy temperatures in the afternoon. You could accidentally make a very nice and fast-acting snake oven. The useful wavelengths of sunlight, by the way, are lost when they are filtered through normal window glass, so putting a glass terrarium in front of a glass window will not increase the natural vitamin production of a snake.

Remember that milksnakes are largely nocturnal in nature, and they do not like bright lights, although they adapt well to normally lighted rooms. They still are most active and more likely to feed when the lights are low.

Water Bowls

Milksnakes require a regular and reliable supply of fresh water. Providing water a captive snake with water is easy. All you need is a bowl that won't tip (one that has a base that is wider than its mouth) and is large enough to provide enough water for drinking—and perhaps an occasional bath—until the next refill, yet not so large that it takes up too much room in the enclosure. Such bowls can be purchased at pet shops. Plastic bowls are lightweight and easy to clean, but some keepers believe that the chemicals used in their manufacture could prove dangerous over time. Stainless steel bowls are inert and literally last forever.

I highly recommend that you change the water every day—and certainly no less often than every other day—cleaning the bowl each time. Milksnakes commonly defecate in their water bowls. Dirty water is a breeding ground for bacteria that can threaten your snake's health. If a snake is thirsty, it will drink regardless of what the water looks or smells like. It's up to you to make sure the water is clean.

Hiding Places

Milksnakes need time to themselves, just like the rest of us, so they don't become stressed by the constant exposure inherent to captive life. Providing them with such places is not difficult. All they really need are four walls and a roof, which of course can be furnished in many forms.

A hiding place can be nothing more than a box with an access hole. Cardboard isn't a good medium because it gets

Plastic plant saucers—which are low-maintenance, easy to cut into, and come in a variety of colors and sizes—make great hiding places for snakes.

dirty fast and will have to be replaced often. But, admittedly, cereal boxes are almost free and are used by many hobbyists who are not especially concerned with the look of the hide box. I wouldn't recommend wood either because it gets dirty quickly and is very difficult to clean. For example, even if you scrub a splotch of feces off a piece of wood, loads of germs will remain in the grain; it is also very difficult to keep mite eggs out of wood.

The safest and most sensible hide box options are those made of plastic or ceramic. An overturned plastic margarine tub of the right size offers a very handy milksnake home. When it needs to be cleaned, all you have to do is remove the snake, and then wash the tub in a sink. Plastic, of course, will not absorb germs the way wood or cardboard would. The only drawback to using plastic is that it doesn't look particularly natural. By contrast, ceramic hide boxes have good heft (are not easily overturned), often have been crafted and painted to look very natural, and are easily cleaned using bleach and heat.

Avoid the habit of lifting your snake's hiding place every time you want to "have a look" at the animal. Remember that this is your snake's private place, and you should properly respect your pet's need for privacy. Snakes often hide because they want to be left alone. Constantly exposing them will only inflict stress and make them feel less comfortable and secure.

Plants

A lot of herpetoculturists consider plants nothing more than decoration and don't bother with them. While it is true that milksnakes don't need plants to survive, a few will do a great deal for an enclosure's visual appeal, and the snakes certainly won't mind (though they may overturn and trample vegetation during their nightly roaming).

Which plants are better—live or artificial? The answer lies in how much time you want to spend caring for live ones. Live plants will need food, water, and suitable lighting (lighting probably not suitable for snakes). If you're a keeper who wants a highly naturalistic setup, then you'll go to the trouble. You can find dozens of suitable types of plants in a garden center, and they're generally inexpensive. My advice is to get plants that have the biggest, floppiest foliage (which will give your snakes extra hiding places) and require the least amount of attention. Live plants in a milksnake's terrarium need to be fairly sturdy because milksnakes occasionally like to climb. With larger specimens, weak plants will quickly be destroyed. Better yet, add some branches to your terrarium.

If you choose artificial plants, make sure you don't buy cheap ones. Buy the plants that are suitable for aquarium displays, ones that will stand up to the humidity without discoloring or decomposing. You will find these types in most pet

Milksnakes are natural climbers, so branches should always be included in their artificial habitat.

shops. The majority of artificial plants sold outside pet shops are purely for display in human environments and almost always contain dyes that will transfer to snakes when they rub against them (especially if they're wet).

Branches

Branches should be in every milksnake enclosure. If they are sturdy enough to handle the weight of your snake, they will provide it with many climbing opportunities. The only drawback is that, being wood, branches don't wash clean and will therefore need to be replaced frequently. Then again, we're talking about branches here—unless you live in an area that is completely devoid of trees, you should be able to get a steady supply of them. However, before adding any wild-collected branch to your enclosure, soak it in a solution of one part household bleach to three parts water for an hour or so, then rinse it until you can no longer smell chlorine.

Cleaning

Making sure your snake's enclosure is clean is tremendously important. A perfectly healthy milksnake kept in a filthy enclosure could develop some nasty illnesses and quickly diminish to the point of no return. The simple fact is that the keeper is solely responsible for the cleanliness of his or her pet's surroundings.

A day or two after each feeding, you should check to see whether your snake has defecated. If it has, put on a rubber glove or use a spoon or cat litter scoop to remove the fecal matter, and clean or replace whatever the matter was sitting on or in. If the fecal matter was in the water bowl, the bowl must also be cleaned. If it was on the substrate, scoop out the soiled portion and replace it with clean substrate. If the substrate is paper toweling, throw out all of it and replace with new toweling.

You should perform a detailed cleaning at least once a month, even if you don't feel that the enclosure needs it. Keep in mind that some of the most threatening organisms are microscopic, so don't be fooled by the thought that the enclosure "looks" clean. A lot of items look clean that really aren't.

Gently rinse your milksnake with warm water whenever you clean out its enclosure.

Before doing any detailed cleaning, remove the snake and place it in a temporary holding bucket or box for the duration of the cleaning. Then remove all enclosure items (plants, hiding places, water bowls), and put them in their own bucket. Now remove the substrate and either wash it thoroughly (gravel) or throw it out (paper towels, newspaper, wood chips).

The container in which your milksnake lives will have to be cleaned as well as everything else. Fill it with warm water, then go over every inch (don't forget those corners!) with a sponge or a very soft scrubbing pad. Rinse with cool water, and dry thoroughly. Add new substrate, and then clean the enclosure items in the same way, making sure they are scrubbed until they're virtually spotless. Now replace those in the aquarium; add fresh water; and then, if you like, give the snake a bath, too. Don't use soap, of course—just some warm water and a sponge (not a scrubbing pad, no matter how soft it is).

Just like everything else in the enclosure, the snakes tend to get dirty. It's no sin to clean them off like you would anything else (not to mention it's good for them). They might squirm around in protest (keep your fingers away from their mouths), but in the end it's for the best. Some specimens will eventually grow accustomed to this process and may even enjoy it after a while. I know I've had a few reach this point.

CHAPTER 6

Feeding

Most milksnakes available to the hobbyist are captive-bred and therefore will usually accept food without fuss. However, some (especially babies) can be stubborn, refusing food until there's almost nothing left of them. Wild-caught specimens of any age can be particularly bad. Before we get any deeper into this topic, let me say that specimens refusing to eat should either be given veterinary attention (looking for a physical cause) or handed over to a more experienced hobbyist who has a better chance of dealing with them. Getting stuck with a milksnake that dies because it won't eat is a nightmarish experience, and in the end you will more than likely be permanently turned off from the whole snake-keeping hobby. Don't let this happen.

Food for Snakes

Milksnakes are strictly carnivorous, meaning they feed only on the flesh of other animals. Their preferred prey is small rodents, lizards, and other snakes. Small rodents—mice, in particular—are probably the food item most commonly offered to rodent-eating snakes and the easiest for a keeper to supply. Rodents are widely available in pet shops, can be purchased in a variety of sizes, from newborns to fully grown adults, and provide plenty of nutrition. They are ideal for milksnakes of any age. They can be offered live, freshly killed, or frozen and thawed. They are generally inexpensive and require little or no maintenance. If you're feeding right away, you simply put them into the snake's enclosure after you get them home. If not feeding right away, you will have to provide the mice with a bit of food, water, and bedding. Even if you only keep mice for a few hours, you will need to provide a sturdy habitat for them—they can quickly gnaw through a cardboard box.

Mouse Stages

Feeder mice have their own terminology that relates to the age of the mouse or rat. A *pinky* is a newborn a few days old that has the eyes closed and lacks any fur. When the fur develops, the mouse becomes a *fuzzy*. As its eyes open and it becomes active though uncoordinated, it is known as a *hopper*. Pinkiess and fuzzies cannot bite and are safe to leave with even a small milksnake. Hoppers can fight back to some extent, and they and any larger mice (or rats, especially) should not be left for long periods with a snake. A rodent left overnight with a snake is likely to chew on the snake and cause serious damage, including deep wounds that could be life threatening or at least disfiguring.

Pinky mice are newborn mice that are more easily consumed by baby or smaller milksnakes.

In the event that you can't find mice or rats at your local pet shop, you can contact a rodent breeder through your local herp society, a reptile magazine, or the Internet. Frozen rodents are commonly sold in bulk quantities and have great practical advantages. First, there's no need for you to spend time and space to maintain a colony—all you need to do is keep them in a freezer. Second, you get a price break when buying in bulk. Finally, frozen-and-thawed mice obviously pose no threat to your snake's health, being unable to attack or fight back.

Unfortunately, some milksnakes simply refuse frozen-and-thawed food items. The only way you're going to find out if your milksnake is of this type is to offer a thawed mouse and see what happens. Even if your snake doesn't take thawed mice at first, it may change its mind later on, so keep trying occasionally; it will be worth the effort in the long run. This is undoubtedly the safest and most functional way to offer food to a milksnake.

When and How Much to Feed

Feeding times, happily, will be dictated by your schedule. Like other captive snakes, milksnakes do not have to have any kind of set internal feeding schedule. In the wild, they are opportunistic, grabbing whatever happens along, whenever it comes along. Their desire to seek out food is motivated purely by hunger, not timing.

It is best to feed your snakes on a regular schedule, however, so that you don't forget when you last fed them. In other words, only feed your snakes on whatever day is most convenient for you, and let them get used to that day. If, for example, you find you have some free time on Saturday evenings, feed

Thawing

Thaw a frozen rodent by putting it in a bowl of warm water for half an hour or so until it is thoroughly thawed; the body cavity must not contain ice crystals. Don't put it in a microwave or conventional oven; the risk of the body exploding is far too great, plus cooking changes the chemistry of the proteins in the muscles, making the food less digestible for a snake.

A Sinaloan milksnake that has recently eaten.

them then. Commonly, milksnakes are fed every week or two weeks, young specimens being fed more often than adults. One simple schedule is to feed when you find feces—this indicates that the snake has digested the last meal and now should be ready for another.

As for amounts, newborn milksnakes can be given one or two pinky mice per feeding, and full-size adults can take one or two adult mice or small rat pups (three or four for the largest specimens).

Overall, it is most important that food be offered regularly. If a snake doesn't accept the food item right away, leave it for a little while. Don't, however, let it sit there all day. Let's face it—if a milksnake doesn't attack a mouse after two or three hours, it simply isn't hungry. There's also a danger that a live mouse or rat could turn on a snake and become the hunter rather than the hunted, inflicting a great amount of damage in the process. In addition, if you're feeding frozen-and-thawed mice and the snake refuses to eat, avoid bacterial contamination by throwing out the uneaten mouse and using a new one the next time you feed.

Stubborn Feeders

If you have a milksnake that steadfastly refuses mice or rats, that doesn't necessarily mean the animal won't take anything—

it may mean it just won't take mice or rats. Again, when working out a problem with a captive snake, use life in the wild as a reference—wild milksnakes, especially juveniles, often eat lizards and other snakes. If possible, try offering these items to your stubborn little friend before declaring it completely unwilling to eat. If in fact it does accept one or the other, great—at least it's eating something. Finicky baby milksnakes that will not even look at a pinky mouse will often eat small skinks and anoles. However, now you've got a new problem—do you really want to sacrifice lizards and/or other snakes for your milksnake?

You do have some options here, the easiest of which is scenting. Collect the shed skins of other snakes and use them to wrap around prekilled rodents of the appropriate size. One hobbyist I know was quite methodical and efficient about this—as soon as one of his other snakes molted, he cut the shed into neat lengths of about 3 or 4 inches, then froze them in airtight bags (to lock in the odors). When it was time to feed his milksnakes, he'd thaw one shed segment for every prekilled mouse that was also thawed, then stuff the mouse into the shed like meat into a sausage casing. Then, as an

Eating isn't a problem for this Sinaloan milksnake.

Fasting

Don't forget that herps do sometimes go through fasting periods and simply don't want or need any food (this is especially common with larger specimens). As soon as you get a new milksnake, weigh it to establish a point of reference. Then, if the animal decides not to eat for a two to three weeks, weigh it periodically. If the animal is not losing any weight, then perhaps it is fasting. If after a month to six weeks it still isn't eating, then consider a vet visit to determine whether the animal is sick. Sometimes just trying different food items and adjusting the snake's terrarium temperature might do the trick.

added measure, he'd rub the shed-wrapped mouse against the body of a live snake to give it a bit more scent. More often than not, this worked. Over time he'd use smaller lengths of shed skin until, eventually, the formerly finicky snake would begin accepting mice without any snakeskin wrapping.

Sometimes you can manipulate a frozen-and-thawed mouse to make it more interesting to the snake. Baby milksnakes often refuse to take pinky mice because they are too large to swallow comfortably. Try offering mouse parts instead, such as a hind leg or a length of tail. Sometimes cutting off the top of the head and exposing the brain of a pinky will interest a snake. This all may be very gruesome, but sometimes it works. You must, of course, use a dead mouse for any of these bloody feeding methods.

If none of these methods work, and your milksnake still refuses to eat, have it checked by a veterinarian or consider giving it to a more experienced keeper with a good record of getting tough cases to feed.

Vitamin and Mineral Supplements

There are now a variety of vitamin and mineral supplements designed specifically for reptiles. They're available in most pet shops that stock herpetocultural goods; but if you can't find any in your local store, try a herp magazine or an Internet source.

These supplements come in two basic forms—powder or liquid. My personal preference has always been the powder, although that's not to say it's more effective than liquid. Whichever one you choose, offer it in limited quantities and on a limited basis. It's like using a spice when you cook—a little bit goes a long way. Remember, your milksnake will receive plenty of nutrition from its staple diet of mice and small rats. Vitamin and mineral supplements are just that—supplements. Sprinkle just a pinch of powder, or apply a drop or two of liquid, on a prekilled or frozen-and-thawed food item just once a month.

Because adult rodents are a complete food—with calcium in their bones and various types of partially digested grains in their bellies—they should give a milksnake all it needs to survive and grow. Using supplements too often, especially vitamin A and calcium, can cause organ damage in a snake.

CHAPTER 7

Handling Milksnakes

Milksnakes may not be in the same category as pythons when it comes to biting, and they are not considered dangerous to handle, but you must remember that they do have teeth and that a large specimen can indeed bite and draw blood. Learning how to properly handle even a small milksnake can prevent accidents.

An albino Nelson's milksnake is large enough to require both hands.

As you can tell by looking through this book, milksnakes fall into two broad categories: small, slender subspecies and larger, stouter subspecies. Most of the milksnake subspecies from the United States are rather small and slender, with narrow heads. Many Mexican and Central American subspecies may be 4 feet long, and some can be well over an inch in diameter, with heads to match. Size has to be considered when handling milksnakes.

Picking Up and Holding

Most small milksnakes are handled rather casually. People tend to pick a milksnake up at midbody with one hand and use the other to control the snake's head. If you find that your snake is frightened by having a hand coming down at it from above and strikes at you, try using a small snake hook to first lift the body a few inches off the bottom of the terrarium. A snake will be less likely to react to the approach of the hook. Once the body is elevated with a hook, you can more easily and safely slip your hand under the body. Larger milks need a bit more care because they can bite hard, and some can be

Snake Hooks

You need few tools when dealing with milksnakes, but it doesn't hurt to purchase a snake hook. Although there are many designs and sizes available, this is basically a handle with a smooth metal hook or angle at the end. The hook is used to lift the middle of the snake's body when first picking it up, giving you a better chance to control the snake as you grab the head. Some Hondurans, for instance, get very nervous when your hand comes at them from above, but they don't object to being partially lifted out of the terrarium by a hook. Small milksnakes are best served by use of small hooks such as models that collapse into a handle, much like a ballpoint pen.

rather vicious. In such a case, the thumb and first fingers of one hand are used to hold the back of the head firmly, and then the other hand supports the rest of the body.

Milksnakes have narrow heads that often are not well separated from the body and have smooth, glossy scales, so they can be rather hard to hold if they are squirmy. Most milksnakes, however, are gentle, don't squirm, and seldom offer to bite once they are used to being handled. Large milksnakes can be very strong snakes, determined to get comfortable in your hands in their own way, so it may take a few minutes before they settle down in a good position.

Dealing with Biting and Spraying

Among keepers, the kingsnakes have developed a reputation for being nippy snakes—even small specimens can be unpredictable. This minor problem just comes with the territory and is generally ignored by keepers. In the case of the larger milksnakes, however, it can present a problem—a big Honduran can cause a bad bite with lots of blood. Just remember to be careful when picking up the snake and give it time to become comfortable in your hands. Squirmy speci-

Hold your snake carefully and be aware of its movements to avoid injury to it or to yourself.

If Bitten

The prospect of being bitten by your pet snake is obviously an unpleasant one. If you should be bitten, the bite can be treated in the home with some soap and water or perhaps a little hydrogen peroxide. A bandage may also be necessary if the wound is particularly bloody (only the bites of the largest subspecies are). Treat the bite as if it were any other puncture or scrape. Making contact with a thorny rosebush is very similar to being bitten by an adult milksnake. However, keep an eye on the wound, and if it doesn't seem to be healing properly, consult your doctor right away.

mens can take up to fifteen minutes before settling.

You also have to keep an eye on the other end of the snake. Milksnakes have large cloacal glands on either side of the vent, or cloaca. These produce a semiliquid, brownish substance that can smell really bad. Disturbed snakes release the contents of the cloacal glands as a defense against predators, but they can also smear the contents along your hands and arms (and sometimes even spray them into your face). Cloacal gland contents are not really feces, but they easily stain many types of clothing and can even eat their way through some thin cotton fabrics unless immediately washed. Some milksnakes have a tendency to spread cloacal content when first picked up and then quickly settle, while others open the glands when they get tired of being held, usually after half an hour to an hour. If you are displaying your milksnake in front of a group, it might be a good idea to "diaper" the snake using a folded paper towel—just in case.

CHAPTER 8

The Most Popular Milksnakes

Although there are more than two dozen described subspecies of the milksnake, not all are equally available in the hobby or equally popular with hobbyists. Certainly an enthusiastic milksnake collector can find at least ten to fifteen subspecies available from various dealers as captive-bred specimens, but the other forms are just rare, seldom available, or too difficult to identify to interest the average hobbyist. About half the subspecies of milksnakes come from Mexico, which has laws restricting or forbidding (depending on species and locality) the export of wild-caught snakes. This means that any Mexican subspecies not already common in the hobby is unlikely to become easier to find in the future. The following subspecies are among the most easily found and most popular, and they are certainly the ones most likely to attract the interest of a beginning keeper.

Black Milksnake, *Lampropeltis triangulum gaigeae*

Large (4 to 5 feet) adults of this subspecies from mountains in Costa Rica and Panama are distinctive because their tri-

The uniquely colored black milksnake.

colored pattern gradually becomes covered with dark pigment, turning them blackish brown. Some specimens seem to be uniformly blackish. It has been suggested that this change to a dark color is due to the black milksnake's cool habitat—dark colors absorb more sunlight faster, which could be an advantage when the snake basks in the cool, foggy mountains in which it lives. Although not common, this subspecies is widely bred by specialists and is hardy, with large hatchlings. Adults may be much more nervous than other milksnakes and inclined to bite, so be careful when first picking up a specimen.

The Central Plains milksnake.

Central Plains Milksnake, *Lampropeltis triangulum gentilis*

Widely distributed over the Great Plains in relatively dry habitats, this is a small (2 feet or less as an adult), slender milksnake, with tiny (under 6 inches) young that may be hard to feed and require lizards during their first months. Even some adults may be able to take only pinky mice. The coloration is the usual red, black, and yellowish white, with all the bands (especially the black) very narrow; some specimens have the black bands incomplete around the back.

The easy-going eastern milksnake.

Eastern Milksnake,
Lampropeltis triangulum triangulum

Found from Minnesota to Massachusetts and south into
Kentucky, this is the common milksnake of the northeastern
United States and the subspecies on which the species name is
based. Adults typically measure from 2 to 4 feet long and
remain slender, with narrow heads. The colors are shades of
gray and reddish brown, while the pattern consists of three
rows of brownish spots (the one over the backbone being the
largest and outlined in black) on a grayish background. Most
specimens have a brown "spearpoint" pattern on top of the
head and neck, much like that of a corn snake. In the southern
part of the range, the colors often become brighter—the grayish background becoming cleaner white or even yellow—
while the blotches become redder and tend to fuse into
uneven bands around the back. The eastern milksnake feeds
mostly on mice and nestling birds. These snakes are widely
sold and bred—though they are not nearly as colorful as the
other milksnakes—and they are easy to care for, with even
hatchlings usually taking pinky mice with few problems. The
eastern milk makes a great beginner subspecies if you are

interested in the U.S. forms but is also interesting if you've become adept with the larger tropical subspecies.

Honduran Milksnake, *Lampropeltis triangulum hondurensis*

One of the most popular milksnakes, the Honduran has a long (4 to 5 feet at maturity), stout, big-headed form. It can be found from Honduras and Nicaragua to Costa Rica. Typical specimens have very wide red bands separated by distinctly orange-yellow bands, the black bands also strongly marked. Through selective breeding, so-called tangerine Hondurans have been produced, in which the red and yellow bands become almost the same color and very bright, separated by reduced black bands. Hatchlings take pinky mice from the start, and adults are very hardy. Some specimens are a bit nervous, and they certainly have the potential for painful bites. Overall, though, this makes a very good choice for the beginning milksnake breeder.

A tangerine Honduran, which is a Honduran in which the red and yellow bands have combined to create bright orange ones.

The slender Louisiana milksnake.

Louisiana Milksnake,
Lampropeltis triangulum amaura

Louisiana milks rank among the smaller subspecies of milksnake, with few adults measuring much over 2 feet in length; hatchlings may be only 5 inches long. Adults are also slender. The red bands are broad, about twice as wide as the black and white (seldom yellow) bands, and the snout varies from solid black to white with reddish blotches. This is a subspecies of the lower Mississippi valley from Arkansas and eastern Texas over much of Louisiana. The subspecies varies greatly in details of color and also intergrades with the adjacent subspecies (scarlet kingsnake and red milksnake). Although the Louisiana milksnake is popular, the small size of the hatchlings means they are very difficult to feed and may require small lizards or even lizard tails for their first dozen meals. Once the snake begins growing, however, it is fairly problem free.

Mexican Milksnake,
Lampropeltis triangulum annulata

Most Mexican milks seen in the hobby actually come from Texas, where the subspecies is fairly common in dry terrain in the southern part of the state. Adults are brightly banded, with the yellow bands relatively narrow and the head black with a wide yellow collar behind it. Few Mexican milksnakes exceed 30 inches in length, but their hatchlings are 8 inches long and relatively stout. Babies and young snakes take pinky mice without many problems. In many ways, this subspecies is more similar to the tropical subspecies than to the other U.S. subspecies.

The brightlly colored Mexican milksnake.

Nelson's Milksnake,
Lampropeltis triangulum nelsoni

Widely bred and popular, Nelson's milksnake (from the Pacific Coast of Mexico) certainly is colorful. The pale bands are yellowish white and very narrow, flanked by wide but

A typically colored Nelson's milksnake.

short black bands and broad, deep red bands. A form of dry habitats, including thorn forests, this subspecies is often more than 3 feet long yet relatively slender. Hatchlings take pinky mice. Recently, albinos and other color variations of the Nelson's milksnake have been bred.

New Mexico Milksnake, *Lampropeltis triangulum celaenops*

One of the smallest milksnakes, with most adults about 14 to 18 inches long, this slender subspecies has a clean, bright color pattern that makes it very desirable to hobbyists. The red areas are broad and bright, sometimes slightly muddy, while the black rings are narrow. White rings tend to be clean white, not yellowish or grayish. The black and white rings continue around the belly, but the red rings often fail to cross. The head is mostly black, with a white snout and often white blotches. This subspecies has a small range in a very dry area (mostly New Mexico, with a few snakes known from Arizona and southwestern Texas), and it spends much of the year underground, coming up only during cool, moist periods. Like other small subspecies, its hatchlings are difficult to feed.

The New Mexico milksnake.

Pale Milksnake,
Lampropeltis triangulum multistriata

This small (adults are generally 18 to 24 inches long), slender milksnake deserves its common name because it often has the weakest colors of all the tricolored milksnakes. The background color tends toward a dusky grayish white—never yellow—while the black rings around the red areas are small or

The pale milksnake, found at the top of the species' geographical range.

even occasionally absent. The red areas are often developed as saddles (not extending around the belly) and may be more orange than red. Typically, neither the red nor black bands circle the belly, which is mostly white. The head is mostly grayish white, with small black areas. Found from Nebraska to Colorado and Montana, often in very dry areas, this is the most northwestern of the milksnakes. Its name has sometimes been spelled multistrata. Comparing an adult pale milksnake with an adult Honduran milksnake really gives you an idea of how variable the milksnake species is over its gigantic range—from Montana to Ecuador.

Pueblan Milksnake,
Lampropeltis triangulum campbelli
Once a rarity, this heavy-set, short-headed subspecies is now widely bred in several color varieties (including apricots, in which the red rings are absent, producing a straw yellow and black snake) and is quite popular. It is a large subspecies—adults often measure nearly 3 feet long—and it can take large pinky mice from hatching. Although wild-colored specimens

One example of a Pueblan milksnake.

are seldom available today, they are distinctive in having the bands all about equally wide, with the black head followed by a wide yellowish white band. This subspecies comes from southern Mexico.

Red Milksnake, *Lampropeltis triangulum syspila*

One of the most widely distributed U.S. subspecies of milksnake, the red milk is found across the center of the country from Indiana to the Dakotas, and south to Oklahoma, and intergrades widely with the subspecies that touch its range.

The commonly kept red milksnake.

Scarlet Kingsnake, *Lampropeltis triangulum elapsoides*

This is a controversial subspecies that is widely distributed over the southeastern United States and is greatly desired by advanced hobbyists. It is also a small (less than 2 feet long), slender subspecies with a small head; in nature, it feeds mostly on lizards, and its small babies generally have to be fed on skinks and skink tails. Even some adults will not accept pinky mice. This is a bright red, yellow, and black burrowing species with a bright red snout. It is usually found in pinelands but sometimes inhabits less sandy area. The scarlet kingsnake is bred in small numbers and, perhaps unfortunately, is often available as wild-caught specimens.

This subspecies is controversial because in many localities it overlaps in range with the brown eastern milksnake, *Lampropeltis triangulum triangulum*, a subspecies with a totally different coloration, pattern, and food choice (taking mice and birds), and does not form intermediates. In other localities it does intergrade, and from southern New Jersey into Virginia, it forms a colorful intermediate once known as the coastal plain milksnake, *L. t. "temporalis."* Because, at least in theory, two subspecies of the same species cannot live in the same area, many field biologists consider the scarlet kingsnake to be a full species (as echoed in the common name) that just occasionally hybridizes with milksnake subspecies. Although the scarlet kingsnake is one of the most beautiful snakes in the United States, it is unfortunately difficult to care for and therefore not recommended for beginners.

The popular yet controversial scarlet kingsnake.

Unlike most Milks, the red is restricted to wide blotches on the center of the back (saddles) outlined by narrow black lines, so the yellowish-white ground color is continuous along the sides. Most of the head is red, with a black and white snout. Certainly one of the most distinctive of the milksnakes, it is widely bred and inexpensive, and it is large enough (adults are often 3 feet long) and heavy enough to feed readily on mice from the moment it emerges from the egg.

Sinaloan Milksnake,
Lampropeltis triangulum sinaloae

The Sinaloan milksnake, found in the lowlands of northwestern Mexico, is widely bred and very affordable. Its large

An example of the mostly red Sinaloan milksnake.

hatchlings take pinky mice with ease, and adults (at 4 feet) are hardy. In color, this subspecies is quite variable, but it usually has very wide orange-red bands separated by short, narrow black bands (often present as isolated spots rather than bands) and narrow yellowish white bands. Selective breeding

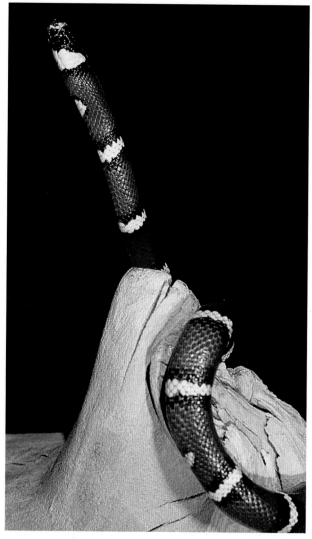

The striking Stuart's milksnake.

has increased the amount of red on this snake and reduced the black and white, so some specimens are almost solid red.

Stuart's Milksnake,
Lampropeltis triangulum stuarti
This brightly colored, stout, large (3 to 4 feet at maturity) milksnake comes from dry forests on the Pacific coast of Central America, between El Salvador and Costa Rica. Both hatchlings and adults are very similar in color, showing few changes with growth. The red rings are quite wide, while the black and white rings are narrow. The scales in the white rings are heavily tipped with black. The head is mostly black except for a white band across the snout. Like several very similar tropical milksnake subspecies (with which it can easily be confused), the hatchlings may be 10 inches long and take pinky mice from the start. Although the Stuart's milksnake is easy to care for and often bred, the subspecies is generally kept by only specialists because it has few advantages over more common tropical subspecies.

Utah Milksnake,
Lampropeltis triangulum taylori
Utah milksnakes are perhaps the hardest U.S. milksnakes to obtain, and they are not considered abundant in their natural

The less-common Utah milksnake.

range (Utah and Colorado). Adults are slender, about 20 inches long, with narrow heads. The black bands and white bands are about equally wide, with the red bands narrow and often split down the center of the back by extensions from the black bands. Commonly, the black and red bands do not extend around the white belly. Most of the white and red scales are tipped with black, giving the snake a dusky appearance. The snout and head are mostly black. Not widely bred in the hobby, this snake is for specialists, not beginners.

Talk to experienced milksnake owners to discover which subspecies is best for you.

CHAPTER 9

Captive Breeding

I n the not-so-distant past, the captive breeding of reptiles was virtually unknown. Now it seems like everyone's doing it. So much is known about the process with some species that you could almost say it has become easy. Fortunately, milksnakes have been captive-bred many times. If you'd like to take a shot at this, follow the information given in the pages ahead and also try to spend some time talking (in person or via the Internet) with people who have already done it. Successfully breeding a pair of snakes is without a doubt one of the most satisfying and rewarding aspects of this hobby. If you've never bred a snake before but are thinking of trying, then I strongly recommend starting with milksnakes. They are ideal for the fledgling breeder.

Only adult milksnakes in peak health will be able to withstand the physical demands of breeding. This especially applies to the females, which must undergo the stress not only

Pushing Milks

Milks attain sexual maturity at roughly two to three years of age. At this point, they should be about 2 to 3 feet in length, depending on the subspecies. Please note that some breeders try to "push" or "rush" their snakes' sexual development through overfeeding. This is not only cruel but also dangerous. I strongly recommend that an owner feed their beloved pets no differently than they would if they weren't breeding them and simply wait until the animals reach the proper size in a natural time frame. If you're in that much of a hurry to breed the snakes, then buy adults to begin with!

of full hibernation or, at the very least, moderate seasonal torpor as applied to tropical lowland subspecies but also of developing and laying the eggs (and often fasting during this time). Unhealthy milksnakes may carry out the act of copulation, but the chances of the females' ultimately laying viable eggs are slim at best.

Sex Determination

Before you begin breeding, of course, you need to know whether you have snakes of both sexes! Sexing milksnakes isn't all that hard. If you look at each snake's tail, on the underside you'll see either one of two things—a sharp inward curving of the body immediately after the cloaca (females) or no particular curving at all (males). The reason for this is that the male's hemipenes are tucked into little pockets in this area, which sort of "fill out" the space. Females, obviously, have no such organs. In other words, at the same general size, the tail of a male milksnake tapers very slowly and is wide over a long area behind the vent, while in a female, the tail tapers quickly and is somewhat shorter than in a male.

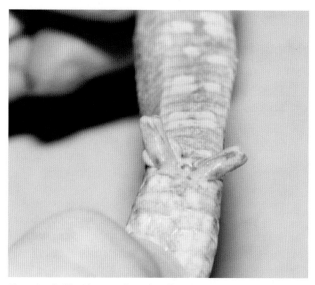

The extended hemipenes of a male milksnake.

A sexing probe being used on a milksnake.

For more precise results, get yourself a stainless steel sexing probe, available at many pet shops that stock herp-related goods. (If you can't find one at a pet shop, order them through a herp magazine or off the Internet.) Probes are available in sets of three or four of different diameters. To use them, first choose the correct size (fairly small for most milksnakes) and then coat the tip of the probe with an inert jelly (check with your local pharmacy). Very gently—I can't stress this enough—insert the probe under the snake's vent scale near the rear left or right side of the vent and slide it toward the tail tip (posterior). Don't push too hard, or you might rupture a pouch. If the probe only goes in the length of about two or three subcaudal scales (the wide paired scales under the tail), you've got a female. If, however, it goes in six to eight scales, you've got a male. Again, be very, very careful with this procedure; you don't want to harm the animal. If you don't feel comfortable trying it, let someone with experience give it a shot and teach you how to do it correctly.

Hibernating Your Milksnakes

Why do you hibernate a milksnake? Basically, it takes a cool period of several weeks to months for the female to mature her eggs and the male to mature his sperm. These sex cells develop best at lower temperatures. A period of hibernation helps ensure that both sexes are physiologically prepared to successfully mate in the spring and produce viable offspring.

Prehibernation

Preparing a milksnake for hibernation (the winterlike cooling period; this process often is called cycling) is crucial not only to the success of your breeding project but also to your snakes' survival. Milksnakes that have not been properly prepared will very likely die during the hibernation interval. Young snakes and snakes that are not being bred generally are not hibernated—the temperature in their terrarium may be dropped a few degrees during the winter and the hours of daylight reduced slightly, but no stress is put on the snakes.

There are two basic steps in cooling: 1) ensuring that the snakes have been well fed; and 2) ensuring there is no undigested food left in their systems. Both points make

Inside Is Best

Milksnakes are best hibernated in indoor containers because it's easier for you to keep an eye on them. Keep in mind that you shouldn't disturb the snakes too much during this time, as it causes added stress. Checking on them once every two weeks is more than sufficient. Hibernating them in outdoor containers makes it very difficult for you to run these crucial checkups. It also increases the chance that they will be found by mice, rats, cats, or larger predators that could work their way into the container and kill your snakes.

Stop feeding milksnakes two weeks prior to hibernation.

sense. Snakes that haven't built up enough body fat will perish in hibernation simply because there isn't enough nutrition in their bodies to sustain them. Undigested food will ferment in their intestines, cause infection, and eventually kill the animals.

Start by increasing feeding by about 25 percent at least six weeks before the animals are due to be hibernated. If they're already in good shape and refuse the extra food, don't worry, but if you can get them to take it, great.

About two weeks before the hibernation begins, cut off the snakes' food altogether. During the last week of this period, place them in a shallow pan of warm water for about two hours each day. That should loosen up their stools and get them to flush everything. The main idea is to have very hefty, yet very empty, snakes when hibernation begins.

Hibernation

Hibernation is, of course, a period of reduced temperature. The right temperature for hibernating milksnakes from the temperate region (North America, east of the deserts or from higher elevations) is around 50 degrees Fahrenheit, give or take two or three degrees. Milksnakes from very warm climates (such as the Mexican and Central American forms)

Lowland Tropical Forms

For tropical lowland subspecies (such as Hondurans, pueblans, blacks, and even Nelsons), a period of full hibernation could be too severe. Subject them to a briefer period at a bit warmer temperature. Instead of dropping their temperature to 50 or 55 degrees Fahrenheit, drop it to about 60 or 62 degrees Fahrenheit. Keep the males and females apart, and hibernate at this temperature for about six weeks. If during this period you see a specimen losing weight, remove it, warm it back up slowly over a day or two, and begin feeding it again. Photoperiod reduction and other climatic factors mirror those for a full hibernation term

can be hibernated a bit warmer, but actually, even desert and tropical montane subspecies come from relatively cool microhabitats. If the temperature goes too much higher than this, your snakes will remain active. If much lower, the snakes may die. The decrease in air temperature should be gradual—perhaps ten degrees a day until you reach the right point. Simply casting the snakes into the cold is too great a shock for many specimens.

The holding container must be aerated, so try using a large plastic tub, complete with lid, and drilling some quarter-inch holes in the sides and top. Bed the container with some sphagnum moss or vermiculite (very slightly moistened), then a few inches of hay or other loose material. Don't use wood shavings because they will inhibit oxygen flow— remember, loose material. Place the snakes inside, and cover them up with more loose material. Then set the box in a dark, quiet area, one where the occupants won't be frightened by a lot of outside activity. Remember, in the wild, milksnakes hibernate underground, and it's fairly quiet down there. During hibernation, not only does the temperature drop but so does the humidity (often to 50 percent or a bit

A full and content red milksnake.

less) and the hours of daylight (commonly six hours rather than the usual eight to twelve).

Hibernation should last about eight to ten weeks. If you hibernate the snakes too long, they could very well die from the stress and lack of food. If you don't hibernate them long enough, their reproductive hormones may not be triggered. They'll still hibernate, but they won't breed (or if they do, the female may lay a bunch of "slugs" rather than fertile eggs).

If, during your biweekly check, you notice that one of your specimens is losing weight fast and looks particularly bad, you should slowly warm it up and start feeding it again. Sometimes a snake simply doesn't respond well to hibernation. It's not common, but you should be aware of the possibility.

Posthibernation

After your milksnakes have finished their time in hibernation, you have to take them out of it the same way you put them in—gradually. Again, an increase of ten degrees per day will do fine. Once they're active again, separate the males and females (many breeders prefer to hibernate the sexes separately in the first place because females are often hibernated longer than males); soak them for a few hours to help empty the stomach of any food residue that could be blocking the intestines; and begin offering food immediately. Needless to say, they're going to be fairly hungry. Make sure the snakes have plenty of privacy during this time and a secure hiding place, because they'll be somewhat disoriented for the first few days. In essence, just make sure they're comfortable and happy.

Mating

This is the big moment—the time when all your hard work pays off. All you really need to do is put a male and female together and let nature take its course. Again, don't do anything to disturb them—just put them together and observe from a reasonable distance. It should be noted here that many professional breeders prefer to introduce the male into the female's enclosure rather than the other way around because males tend to be a bit territorial and may try to harm any "intruders." In nature, males also generally track down females by following scent trails deposited by females ready to mate.

If both snakes are interested in mating, you'll be able to tell right away. The male, his tongue flicking in and out madly, tasting the female's airborne pheromones (sexual scents produced by glands between the scales), will glide along and over her body and try to entwine their tails. If the female is receptive to his advances, she will lift her tail, exposing her vent, and the male will insert one of his two hemipenes. After copulation begins, the two will most likely lie nearly motionless; the entire act could take anywhere from a few minutes to a few hours. Copulation is finished when the snakes part ways. It's a good idea to put males and females together again every few days in the hope that repeated breedings will occur. This will almost guarantee successful fertilization of the female's eggs.

Pregnancy and Egg Laying

After you're sure you've got a gravid, or pregnant, female (it should become fairly obvious after about three weeks—you'll see the snake begin to "bulk up" in the posterior part of the

A female albino Nelson's milksnake protects her eggs.

body), you should set her up in her own enclosure. You'll need to take special care of her during the pregnancy.

Milksnakes are oviparous, meaning they are egg layers. Normal gestation (fertilization to laying) for this species is anywhere from forty to sixty days, but as few as twenty-two and as many as sixty-five days have been recorded. You'll need to make special preparation for the egg laying.

Care of a Gravid Female

If the pregnant milksnake will accept food, offer it slightly more frequently than normal. Remember that the developing eggs need nutrition from her, so she'll need as much as she can get. If she refuses food, don't be alarmed—this is fairly normal. If, however, she goes on a severe fast and obviously begins losing weight, take her to a veterinarian or a professional herpetologist. Whatever you do, don't handle a gravid female unless necessary. She's stressed enough as it is—adding more stress could very easily interrupt the development of the eggs or cause the mother to lay them prematurely. Be especially careful to keep her enclosure clean, and give her plenty of clean water.

No Egg Box?

If you fail to provide an egg box in which the female can lay, you probably will not get viable eggs. The eggs may be scattered around the terrarium, where they will quickly dry out and die. If they are laid in the water bowl (as often happens), the embryos drown in a few minutes, and again, you lose the eggs. The worst that can happen is that the female simply refuses to lay her eggs because there is no suitable nest, and she holds them in the body so long that they begin to calcify and can no longer be laid. This results in what is known as egg-binding or dystocia, which can lead to the death of the female and certainly will need prompt veterinary attention—and you still lose the eggs. Please, spend the extra time to supply a good egg box!

Egg Laying

You need to provide an egg box. This is basically a container in which the female can lay her eggs when the time comes. Almost any small box will do, but I've always preferred a plastic container with a lid. The lid should have a hole of the correct size (large enough for the female to enter) cut through it. In truth you don't really need to use a lid at all, but I like to provide one for milksnakes because they are so secretive by nature. You may discover the female spending a lot of time in the box long before the eggs are due. The egg box should be bedded with the standard substrates for egg laying: moistened vermiculite or sphagnum moss, both of which are available at most garden-supply stores and some pet shops.

When the female begins laying her eggs, don't disturb her. Once you're certain she's finished, gently remove her from the egg box, then carefully remove the box itself. If the eggs were laid while you were out, you may come home to find the female coiled around them in a protective posture. This is normal for many snakes, but there is no evidence that a mother milksnake ensures a successful incubation period by remaining with her clutch, and she won't defend it by attacking you. Gently remove her as a precursor to removing the egg box.

Give the female about twenty-four hours to recover from the traumatic experience, then begin offering food again. It's very important to both her physical and mental health that she deal with as little stress as possible.

Care of Eggs

Correct temperature and humidity levels for developing eggs are pretty much the same as they are for the snakes during their "active" season—about 78 degrees Fahrenheit and about 100 percent humidity. Commercial incubators are widely available today, or you can make one from a foam box and a submersible aquarium heater. One crucial point about the eggs—they must remain in the exact position in which they were laid. Turning them over in any way will smother the embryos. One way to ensure that the eggs remain in the proper position is to put a dot on the top of each egg using a water-based marker.

Set the incubator in a spot where it will not be disturbed. Check the bedding every few days to make sure it stays moist; if you add water, don't get the eggs wet. If you see any mold or fungus on an egg, carefully remove it using a dampened paintbrush. Bad eggs, it should be noted, will shrivel and discolor very quickly. These should be thrown out immediately. They will develop fungus that could spread to the other eggs.

The Babies

It takes about fifty to seventy-five days for milksnake eggs to hatch. Around day forty-five, you should start keeping an eye out for the first little slit where a baby snake is trying to find his or her way out. There may be some temptation to "help" the little snake get out of its shell, but this urge should be resisted. Any interference in the hatching process could easily kill the animal. The snake will slice a small opening in the shell with the aid of a tiny egg tooth (which will disappear after a few days), then push its way out. A small yolk sac may still be attached to the snake, but it will be used up in a day or two, leaving a short vertical

A baby albino Nelson's milksnake and its mother.

umbilical scar that will seal over and gradually disappear.

Take the babies out of the incubation container only after they are moving about freely. They should then be set up in their own enclosure and offered food (pinky mice, mouse parts, and tiny lizards or lizard tails are the most common items) immediately after their first molt, which generally happens within a week to ten days of hatching. Baby milksnakes commonly have a voracious appetite, so feeding shouldn't be a problem if you can find food small enough to be readily taken.

The most common problem with baby milksnakes is that the young of the smallest subspecies (such as the Louisiana milksnake and the scarlet kingsnake) are just too tiny to take normal foods. A pinky mouse is gigantic compared with the head of one of these milksnakes. Keepers often consider such small subspecies to be material for specialists only. For the tiny babies, you may have to resort to feeding baby anoles or ground skinks (*Scincella*), both of which may be available frozen from Internet dealers. Expect a fairly high mortality rate with these subspecies, as some never do eat.

Fortunately, however, the babies of Honduran, Mexican, Sinaloan, and similar popular milksnakes are large and aggressive and will take pinky mice or mouse parts within a week of hatching. If you are a beginning breeder, start with these larger forms before trying the tiny ones.

Young milksnakes grow quickly and should about double their length each year for the first two years, when they become sexually mature. As they grow, they become easier to feed on standard foods and also become hardier and less subject to diseases and parasites. Of course, a captive-bred milksnake should be subject to few of these kinds of problems, making them among the hardiest captive snakes. This durability, combined with their bright colors, is the secret of their success.

CHAPTER 10

Hybrid Milksnakes

Because successfully breeding milksnakes and other kingsnakes has become so commonplace, some hobbyists have been challenged to try tougher and tougher projects with these snakes. One aspect of breeding that has produced controversial results is the breeding of hybrids.

What Is a Hybrid?

Technically, a hybrid is the result of interbreeding two distinct species. If two subspecies of a single species are interbred, the offspring are technically intergrades, not hybrids. There is no doubt that any two subspecies of milksnake—all twenty-five of them—could be interbred in captivity to produce intergrades with characters somewhat between the two parents. In fact, in some taxonomic philosophies, natural intergradation in which two subspecies come into contact is considered proof that the snakes truly represent subspecies, not species. Producing intergrade milksnakes is not a great problem, as the subspecies share virtually all the same genes and have the same chemical processes in place that time the development of the embryo. You might have a physical problem interbreeding a tiny, slender subspecies such as *L. t. amaura* with a large, stout one such as *L. t. hondurensis* (which might mistake the other for lunch!), but in theory, this crossing is not a problem genetically. The offspring also should be generally fertile and pass on their mixed genes. Hobbyists today sometimes interbreed three or even four subspecies of milksnake, especially albino varieties, to produce some very strange-looking milks.

Hybrids are another story because, at least in theory, if two snakes are of different species, they have significant differences in their genes, often including the genes that control the chemistry that times development of the embryos. They are considered distinct species in the first place because, over time, mutations have changed the chemistry of their genes to the point at which there are built-in factors preventing interbreeding. This means that although a female may become gravid after mating with a male of another species, the embryos may never develop fully. This is why, until recently, taxonomists considered the ability of two species to hybridize in nature (not in the terrarium) to be proof that they were actually subspecies, not species. Today, however, the philosophy has changed, and hybridization between two species is not considered taxonomically significant—just a primitive character or feature with little meaning.

We know from experience that virtually all the larger and more common species of the tribe Lampropeltini can be forced to interbreed in captivity, producing hybrids. These hybrids may be infertile (thus the line would have to be rebred each time a new generation is wanted), partially fertile (only males or only females may produce living, active eggs or sperm), or completely fertile (both sexes are able to pass on their mixed genetic makeup). This means that many or most of the species of *Lampropeltis, Pantherophis, Scotophis,* and *Pituophis* (crossings of which produce the greatest number of successful hybrids) must be genetically very similar for two specimens not only to mate but to produce living offspring that can mature.

Crosses between species currently lodged in a single genus are known as intrageneric or interspecific hybrids, while crosses between species currently placed in different genera (for example, *Lampropeltis* and *Pantherophis*) are called intergeneric crosses. In theory intrageneric crosses should be easier to produce than intergeneric crosses because there should be fewer genetic differences between species of a single genus than species of two different genera, but in reality this distinction doesn't seem to exist. However, I've never heard of crosses between the major genera mentioned here and the smaller, more obscure genera of the tribe Lampropeltini such as *Arizona* (glossy snakes),

A hybrid between a Sinaloan milksnake and a California kingsnake is called a Sinacal. This particular Sinacal is an albino.

Cemophora (scarlet snakes), and *Rhinocheilus* (long-nosed snakes). But it's probably just a matter of time before such hybrids are produced.

Dangers of Hybridizing Snakes

Before discussing how a breeder can create hybrids, we should discuss the dangers of hybridizing snakes and whether it should even be attempted. Hybridizing milksnakes and other snakes is not a widely accepted activity. Hybrids are generally only tolerated in the hobby and seldom looked upon highly. Many breeders just don't see the point of hybridizing snakes and instead see some of the problems.

Some hybrid milksnakes are beautiful animals—especially when one of the parents is an albino or otherwise very colorful variety (usually called a morph)—but this is the exception rather than the rule. Many hybrids are unattractive or superficially look much like one parent or the other. Hybrid hatchlings also run a large chance of having crooked spines, incomplete scale development, irregular patterns, and other problems that are likely due to differences in the genes timing their development. Most hybrid combinations produce few living offspring, and then fewer of these survive to adulthood and are fertile.

One major problem is that you have to accept the breeder's word as to what is the background of any hybrid. There is no way to look at a hybrid and determine its parents, especially in second-generation hybrids in which snakes are recrossed to a parent or crossed to another hybrid. Experience tells us that taking the unsupported word of a dealer can lead to problems.

Scientifically, there is another major problem: hybrids may be rebred into a pure species line without being detected superficially and add genes of another species into that line. For example, if you hybridize a corn snake and a pueblan milksnake and then rebreed the hybrid back to its pueblan milksnake parents, you add corn snake genes to the pueblans. After one or two breedings, all superficial signs of a corn snake in the inheritance may disappear, but the genes of the corn snake are conserved and spread into all the pueblan milksnakes that result from the breedings. Your pueblan milksnake breeding line is no longer pure, even if all the snakes you produce look like normal pueblans. After a few snakes are sold back and forth between different breeders and hobbyists, the presence of corn snake genes could easily be forgotten or ignored.

Now assume that pueblan milksnakes become very rare in nature and a group decides to try to reintroduce pueblans into their natural range. (This, of course, happens.) They gather nice pueblans preserved by captive breeders and return them to Mexico. When checked in a decade or so, they might find that all the pueblans in the natural range are now just a bit different from the original natural pueblans—the corn snake genes have reappeared in the superficial look of the snakes, and

Multiple Breedings

There is considerable evidence that female snakes can store sperm from a mating for long periods of time, perhaps well over a year. If the female has bred before, there is a chance that some or all of the eggs produced will have been fertilized by the male of the previous mating, not by the male chosen for your attempt at a hybrid.

true pueblans now no longer exist in nature at all. The possibility of contamination of natural gene pools by hybrids is real—at least real enough to worry some scientists.

Finally, hybrids are strictly domestic animals—they do not exist in nature. (Natural hybrids among different species are virtually unknown.) They carry the bacteria, viruses, and worms that other domestic snakes carry—often a very different assortment than would be found in nature. The hybrids might also display different degrees of tolerance to these parasites than their parent species do. Common bacteria could pass through a hybrid and in the process become completely immune to all treatments now available for the disease they produce in other snakes. Even new combinations might be possible, because bacteria and viruses manage to exchange genetic material. If hybrids escape, they could carry into nature unexpected diseases that could badly affect the parent species.

There are no laws or rules prohibiting hybridizing milksnakes and other snakes, and none are likely to come into play soon. In fact, more and more hobbyists are becoming interested in hybrids. The decision to breed hybrids is yours, but you should be aware of the major problems they may create.

Making a Hybrid

Hybrids between milksnakes and various other species in the listed genera are usually produced by simply fooling

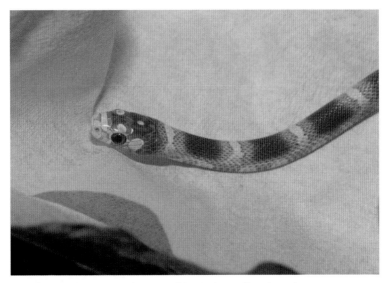

This albino Sinacorn is a combination of the Sinaloan milksnake and the corn snake.

snakes in the midst of mating frenzy. Be aware, however, that not all hybrid matings are equal: although some pairings have a good chance of success, many do not. Below are instructions for how to go about the process of creating hybrids and some information on which pairings are the most likely to succeed.

The Process of Hybridization

After overwintering each species correctly, the breeder feeds and soaks the specimens and prepares them for mating. A male milksnake is placed with a female of the same species, often in the darkness of a cloth bag. The male smells out the female, courts her, and then begins inserting his hemipenes to pass sperm. At that moment, when this activity can be felt through the bag, the breeder removes the female and replaces her with an overwintered, ready female of a different species, preferably one that was in the process of mating with a male of her own species. The male milksnake will continue to mate, even if he must force the female, and will pass sperm. As soon as the snakes decouple (which may be an hour or more, remember), the pair is separated and the female is treated as any other potentially gravid specimen of her species. If the mating can be repeated two or three times, the odds of fertile eggs are greatly increased, but this often is not possible. As long as the two snakes being hybridized are of similar size and are equally prepared for mating, success is quite possible.

If the female is truly gravid and lays eggs, the breeder usually will incubate them as if they were of her species. Because incubation procedures for eggs of the common species of Lampropeltini are similar anyway, there is seldom a problem.

The Unpredictability of Hybridization

Not all hybrid matings are equal: the results of crossbreeding are unpredictable because so many genes are involved. In some cases, breeders have found that crossings are sex restricted. Thus, only male milksnakes might mate successfully with only female corn snakes (*Pantherophis guttata*), not the other way around (female milks might not successfully mate with male corns). Little has been published about this because, in order to corner the market, commercial breeders choose to keep successful mating techniques secret and hobbyists seldom publish details of breedings. Some

Jungle Corns

Corn snakes *(Pantherophis guttata)* hybridize with California kingsnakes *(Lampropeltis getula californiae)* to produce so-called jungle corns. One of the first hybrid combinations produced in quantity, these hybrids are usually fertile. Often, jungle corns can then be hybridized with larger milksnake subspecies such as Hondurans and Sinaloans to produce very attractive and unusual-looking second-generation hybrids.

species pairings also work better than others. It long has been known, for instance, that most species of *Lampropeltis* can hybridize with corn snakes (*Pantherophis*) and black rat snakes (*Scotophis*) to produce fertile hybrids. Because few hybrids between milksnakes or other *Lampropeltis* species and gopher snakes (*Pituophis*) have been produced, it is likely that species of *Pituophis* are more remote genetically from *Lampropeltis* than are the species of *Pantherophis* and *Scotophis*, which do hybridize. Even *Pituophis* by *Pantherophis* crosses are unusual, although possible—crossing a gopher snake with a corn snake results in a turbocorn, usually bred from albino parents.

Some Common Hybrids

Using the word *common* to describe any milksnake hybrid combination is really misleading because these hybrids are not easily produced, are often extremely expensive to purchase, and are not widely available. The following are some of

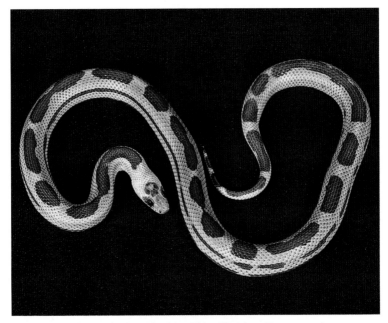

A Pueblacorn—the result of crossing a Pueblan milksnake with a corn snake.

the more often bred combinations at the moment. Perhaps in the future they will actually become common.

- Sinacals are hybrids of Sinaloan milksnakes (*L. t. sinaloae*) by California kingsnakes (*L. getula californiae*), especially albinos.
- Corndurans are hybrids of corn snake (*Pantherophis guttata*) by Honduran milksnake (*L. t. hondurensis*) crosses. When unusually colored varieties (morphs) of either parent are used, strikingly colored hybrids can result.
- Brookians are an uncommon and odd cross of the "*brooksi*" variety of the Florida subspecies of the common kingsnake (*L. getula floridana*) with a Pueblan milksnake. They look much more like the kingsnake parent than the milksnake parent.
- Clown kings represent a complex second-generation hybrid combination. These pretty but variable snakes carry the genes of albino Nelson's milksnake (*L. t. nelsoni*), the milksnakelike "*thayeri*" variety or sub-species of the Mexican kingsnake (*L. mexicana*), and the apricot morph of the Pueblan milksnake (*L. t. campbelli*). With such a strange genetic background, it is almost impossible to predict what progeny will look like.
- Sinacorns, as you might expect, result from crossing a Sinaloan milksnake with a corn snake.
- Pueblacorns are obviously the progeny of a Pueblan milksnake crossed with a corn snake.
- Painted kings and imperial kings represent what you get when crossing Pueblan milksnakes with California kingsnakes. When the first-generation hybrid offspring are bred back to either parent, the percentage of genes of that parent increases in the offspring, resulting in different appearances (and breeder names) with coming generations.

Noted in dealer ads also are unnamed crosses of California kingsnakes with Pueblan milksnakes and Pueblan milksnakes with Ruthven's kingsnakes (*L. ruthveni*). Honduran milk-snakes have also been successfully crossed with Texas rat snakes (*Scotophis obsoleta*). It seems likely that many other combinations are being tried, sometimes successfully.

Why Hybridize Snakes?

From the commercial breeder standpoint, hybrids mean money. They require a lot of effort to produce, with even successful matings leading to few eggs and even fewer hatchlings that may never mature. Some hybrids are unattractive and almost unsaleable, but some are beautiful. This means that successful hybrids bring in big bucks and are worth the effort.

The average hobby breeder may have become bored with just producing another litter of Honduran milksnakes or Mexican milksnakes that he or she feels is just taking up terrarium space. The thrill of trying something more difficult—and vaguely Frankensteinish in scientific content—may be hard to resist. And if you do happen to produce a good hybrid, you can probably sell it for a nice profit.

Scientifically, little is gained from hybridizing members of Lampropeltini. Today's taxonomic philosophies hold that hybrids should be expected even under some natural conditions whenever species are somewhat related, so the fact that two species will successfully mate when placed in a bag is not exciting and proves nothing. Fifty years ago, hybrids excited scientists, but today the idea of hybridization is sort of passé.

CHAPTER 11

Diseases and Disorders

Milksnakes are hardy snakes, and even the hatchlings of the larger subspecies do very well in the terrarium. However, like any pet, they occasionally have problems. Most of them are easy to handle with a bit of patience, but some require that you work with a veterinarian who is experienced with reptiles. The best way to ensure the health of your pet snakes, however, is to avoid buying a diseased animal.

Study your snake when it's healthy so that you'll be able to know when it's not.

Diseases, Disorders, and Their Signs

Before you buy, make as certain as you can that the snake is healthy. Look for obvious problems: patchy skin, cloudy eyes, growths around the mouth, difficulty breathing, dried feces around the vent, pustules under the scales, or scales missing from the tip of the tail. These can be signs of some of the serious health problems listed below.

Mites

Mites can often be found on snakes purchased from pet shops (and from breeders, for that matter), because mites are very difficult to eradicate from a commercial establishment. Snake mites are tiny relatives of spiders and are smaller than a pinhead and often translucent. They turn brown to reddish after they feed on the blood and lymph of a snake, sticking their mouthparts into soft areas around the eyes and between the scales. They spend the day in tiny crevices in the cage or even outside the cage (they move quickly and flourish even under dry conditions) and under debris. At night, they come out to feed. Heavy snake mite infestations can drain a small snake of significant amounts of blood and be highly stressful, sometimes causing death. Any pet shop that sells snakes should sell preparations to kill mites, as well, but a quick bath in olive oil (followed by a

Find a Vet

Veterinarians are necessary to successfully treat more complicated and dangerous problems with milksnakes. You may never need to go to a vet—though it's a good idea to have a newly purchased snake checked out by one—but you certainly should be aware of veterinarians with reptile experience in your neighborhood in case a problem should come up. Start by calling local veterinarians listed in the phone book or online and asking them about their opinion of snakes as pets and any experience they may have with them. Few vets have much training with exotic pets such as snakes. But there are some who keep snakes themselves and will be happy to examine your specimen after purchase to determine its general health. A good veterinarian is worth the money you have to pay for his or her services.

Shedding in patches can be a sign of and/or result in a serious medical problem.

careful rubbing down with paper towels to remove the oil) is just as effective, as long as the cage is also completely sanitized. Many commercial miticides may harm or even kill young milksnakes, especially those of the smaller subspecies, so be careful and try not to purchase a snake with mites.

Mouthrot

Mouthrot (infectious stomatitis) is a serious bacterial disease of snakes and lizards that is often seen in wild-caught snakes being sold in shops. The inside of the mouth, including the jaws and the tissues of the roof of the mouth, becomes covered with little white to yellow pimples that congeal into a thick coat that can literally cover the teeth and then eat away the tissues. A snake with mouthrot will not eat and can spread the disease to other snakes. Serious infections can result in death. A veterinarian will carefully remove some of the diseased tissue and treat the snake using antibiotics, but often the bacteria are resistant to treatment and the snake becomes terminal even with care. It is important that you check the mouth of any milksnake you plan on purchasing—you can do this in most cases by watching the animal eat, when the mouth will be widely open during swallowing.

Shedding Problems

Persistently patchy sheds could be a sign of a more important problem requiring veterinary attention—perhaps a vitamin deficiency. Some snakes have a problem shedding the eyecaps—the round bits of transparent skin (the spectacles or brilles) over the eyes. If these are allowed to accumulate, the snake's sight will suffer, as will its appetite. Stuck eyecaps can be carefully removed—preferably by a veterinarian—with moist cotton swabs or even adhesive tape.

URIs

Respiratory diseases, commonly called colds and pneumonia, are often seen in milksnakes kept in air-conditioned premises and crowded quarters. They also develop in snakes kept too dry or too moist, and they are often quite contagious. A snake with an upper respiratory infection (URI) commonly breathes hard through an open mouth. The snake may be lethargic and often has fluid around the nostrils (a "runny nose"). Most URIs can be treated using antibiotics, but this can be expensive and not always successful, as stressed snakes often redevelop the problem every few months. The best idea is to not purchase a snake that may have a URI.

Emergency Kit

It's a good idea to keep a few standard items around the snake room. A basic emergency kit could include bottles of rubbing alcohol (70 percent) and hydrogen peroxide, a tube of povidone iodine (such as Betadine) for treating minor cuts and scrapes, cotton swabs, a pair of good tweezers (forceps), and a pair of small scissors.

Always quarantine your new snake, no matter how healthy it seems to be.

Quarantine

Quarantine any new purchase for at least a month before adding it to your collection of other snakes or lizards. A contagious disease or parasite could spread to your other pets and create havoc in just a few days. Keep the snake in a small but comfortable terrarium with the proper temperature and humidity and lots of hiding places, preferably in a room separate from the other snakes to help prevent transmission of air-borne bacteria, fungi, and viruses. This is also a good time to let the milksnake acclimate to new keeping conditions and perhaps new foods. If nothing unusual happens by the end of the month, it is almost certainly safe to add the new purchase to your collection.

Milksnakes, especially adults, are hardy animals and not especially subject to diseases if they are kept well and fed well. Stress, however, can bring on many problems—some serious, some not—and pet shop and breeding establishment conditions are often stressful. Buy a healthy snake, have a veterinarian look it over if at all possible, and keep it well—this is the formula for maintaining a healthy, vital milksnake.

Record Keeping

Keeping records is tremendously important. There will come a time—I guarantee it—when you'll need past information for reference and wish you'd kept track of everything. If your milksnake gets sick, your vet will ask a lot of questions about what's been happening with the animal lately. The more information you can provide, the better the chances of the animal's being treated successfully.

In addition, it is both educational and fascinating to see certain patterns develop over the course of your milksnake's life. You'll be surprised what you can learn simply by building up a prolonged profile of the snake's activities. Finally, no one can debate the value of meticulously kept records. Maybe someday you'll meet and befriend another enthusiast. You can bet that person will be grateful if you share all the records you've kept. Such information will be a great help in allowing a new keeper to more quickly understand how his milksnake is likely to react to different situations and foods.

So what are "the basics" you should record? Let common sense be your guide. Some things are obvious—when a snake eats, what it ate, and how much it ate; when it defecates; and when it sheds. If the snake throws up its food (which many captive reptiles do when they're stressed), you'll want to write that down. Note if your snake refused food, as well. Anything to do with breeding should, of course, be recorded (matings, egglayings, and so on). Again—use common sense. I like to write down anything and everything, never assuming I already know what information will or won't be important later on. If you cover all your bases, you'll always be safe.

PIT Tags

Recently the use of passive induced transponder (PIT) tags has become possible with the larger and more expensive milksnakes. A PIT tag is a tiny glass or plastic capsule (about the size of a large grain of rice) containing a microchip that is coded with a unique identification number and responds to a special electronic reader. A veterinarian injects the tag into the abdominal cavity of the snake using a special syringe. No surgery is required, and the snake does not feel any pain or side effects from the tag. When the reader is passed over the snake, it sends out a radio signal that turns on the microchip, and the chip's number is displayed on a tag reader. The tag is permanent and lasts for the lifetime of the snake. The snake is not deformed in any way.

The advantage of PIT tags is that the snake is permanently identifiable if lost, escaped, or stolen. The unique number of the tag goes into a registry that can be accessed by vets with the proper readers. Lost snakes can be legally identified even years after a theft. In some states, it is now possible to legally keep native milksnakes and other reptiles only if they have been PIT tagged for future reference—in these states, untagged snakes in a collection are considered illegal even if legally purchased in another state. It is possible to PIT tag almost any snake, but the larger subspecies are generally easier and safer to tag. Check with your veterinarian for more details. The cost of PIT tagging has dropped greatly over the past few years, and the procedure should now be in the budget range of any hobbyist.

CHAPTER 12

Almost Milksnakes

W hen most herp hobbyists think of milksnakes, they think of the so-called tricolored snakes—those with bands of black, red, and white or yellow around the body. Although this type of pattern is indeed distinctive for most (but not all) milksnakes, it is also shared by some closely related species and by some species a bit less-closely related. It seems appropriate to discuss some of these here, especially because they often share keeping and breeding requirements with the milksnake.

California Mountain Kingsnake, *Lampropeltis zonata*

Another gorgeous tricolored kingsnake that is much like a milksnake at first glance, the California mountain kingsnake is restricted to the western coastal states from the Washington-Oregon border area south through central and coastal California and then into Baja California, Mexico. It is rather heavy-bodied, about 20 to 40 inches long (sometimes up to 4 feet), and its snout and the top of its head are black back to at least the level of the eyes. Although similar species appear to be ringed in white, black, and red, California mountain kings are a bit different, being essentially black-and-white-ringed snakes with small to very wide red spots inside the black rings. Commonly, the red spots from each side connect over the backbone to make full red rings around the snake, but in almost any group of snakes, you can expect some to have a few wide black rings with little red visible. The background varies greatly with age and locality, from glossy white through grayish white with darker scale tips to bright yellow. The whitish rings remain narrow all the way down to the belly, not widening out on the lower side as in milksnakes. As many as seven subspecies have been recognized in the past, but there is so much variation that no one can agree on how to use the names. Recent DNA studies have cast doubt on the validity of many of the subspecies. Very popular and often expensive snakes in the hobby, California mountain kings are protected through much of their range at the state or national (Mexico) level, so be sure to purchase only legally captive-bred specimens.

The California mountain kingsnake.

Keeping adult California mountain kings is rather simple, and they can be set up much like milksnakes from the drier parts of the range. Give them a simple terrarium with moderate undertank heating (up to about 80 degrees Fahrenheit is fine) and a weak basking light, as well as lots of cover. Most

Triads

Scientists call the groups of black and red bands in tricolored kingsnakes triads because, when fully developed, a single black ring is completely divided by a red ring (thus black-red-black). Each triad is separated from the next by a white to yellow band. The number of triads has been used to define subspecies in California mountain kings but is also very variable in any population.

adults bask each day, so the snakes can be used for display specimens. Adults take mice of appropriate size.

Breeding takes place in the spring after several months of lowered temperatures. Almost all populations of this species need distinctly lower wintering temperatures than more eastern tricolored kings do to produce fertile eggs in the spring. The suggested overwintering range is between 40 and 50 degrees Fahrenheit, almost ten degrees lower than that for related species, so it may be necessary to remove the snakes from their terrarium in the winter and place them in a cooler area than the snake room. Three to nine eggs are typically laid and can be incubated much as are milksnake eggs.

A major problem with breeding this snake is that the hatchlings and juveniles often demand lizards, rejecting mice. Provide hatchlings with baby lizards (ground skinks, *Scincella lateralis*, and fence lizards, *Sceloporus*, of all types are accepted) at first and gradually wean them to lizard-scented pinkies and then larger mice. This is one of the few snake species in which individuals have lived for more than twenty years in the terrarium.

Ruthven's Kingsnake, *Lampropeltis ruthveni*

Often called the Queretaro kingsnake in the terrarium hobby, this species belongs to the confusing group of snakes related to the gray-banded kingsnake, *Lampropeltis altena*, from western Texas and northern Mexico, and the Mexican kingsnake, *Lampropeltis mexicana*, from northern to central Mexico. These latter species are grayish with wide red blotches across the back, edged with black, the belly being black and gray to black and yellowish. The Mexican kingsnake has a very milksnakelike color phase or subspecies called Thayer's kingsnake, but an even more milksnakelike

A Ruthven's kingsnake—a snake often confused with the milksnakes in its natural habitat.

form is Ruthven's kingsnake, from central Mexico. In fact, telling this species from milksnakes found in the same area is almost impossible without counting the number of scales on the belly. Fortunately for hobbyists, most Ruthven's kingsnakes sold in the hobby are albinos or hybrids with the gray-banded kingsnake, so the problem seldom arises.

Natural Ruthven's kingsnakes are like Mexican subspecies of milksnake (such as *Lampropeltis triangulum arcifera* and *L. t. nelsoni*) in being 30 to 36 inches long, rather stout, with a black snout and top of the head. The body is ringed with wide, dull-red bands separated by narrower black and grayish white bands, the bands sometimes breaking up and becoming confused on the belly. The edges of the rings are cleanly defined, the black not wandering into the red area. Often, there are reddish blotches on the snout. Scale counts are important for distinguishing this species—specimens have twenty-one to twenty-five rows of scales around the back (more than many milksnakes) and 182 to 196 ventral or belly scales (fewer than milksnakes in the same area). The species is found in a broad arc across western central Mexico northwest of Mexico City. Albinos usually show the red as brilliant, clean red rings separated by pinkish rings (representing the black rings) and glossy white areas. Often, the red rings are broken across the back and are very irregular at their edges, but there is much variation.

Regardless of its taxonomy, Ruthven's kingsnake is easy to keep and is similar to gray-banded kingsnakes in its requirements. It does well in a simply decorated terrarium with undertank heating and a weak basking light (which may seldom be used) and lots of cover. Adults take mice of appropriate size, but hatchlings may demand lizards, or at least lizard-scented pinkies, and sometimes never feed.

Scarlet Snake, *Cemophora coccinea*

This is a colorful burrowing snake often confused with the milksnake. At first glance, it is indeed similar to several milksnake subspecies, its white back being crossed by broad red rings bordered on each side by narrower black bands, resulting in the usual white-black-red-black-white pattern

An example of the scarlet snake—a difficult snake for hobbyists to keep.

typical of the young adult milksnake. A closer look, however, shows that the red and black "rings" are actually saddles that do not extend all the way down the sides of the snake and do not cross the belly, which is almost unmarked white. The snout is also more pointed than that of any milksnake and is red rather than the usual white or black milksnake (but remember that the very similar scarlet kingsnake also has a red snout). Adults are generally between 15 and 25 inches long and remain slender, with narrow heads. Hatchlings are bright pinkish red with narrow black bands against a clean white background, but with age, the red areas darken to a solid red and then often a muddy brownish red against a grayish white background heavily flecked with darker gray scales. This species is found in areas with loose soils from southeastern Texas to southern Florida and north to New Jersey and Missouri. Its burrowing habits mean that it comes above ground mostly after heavy rains. It is seldom collected.

Many hobbyists have tried to keep scarlet snakes, but relatively few have succeeded. Not only are these snakes small, nocturnal, and rather delicate, but they are also notoriously difficult to feed. Although specimens in nature occasionally have been seen to feed on small frogs, snakes, lizards, and even mice, the scarlet snake's preferred diet seems to be turtle and snake eggs. In captivity, few specimens will take any food other than eggs. Turtle and snake eggs are seldom available on a regular basis, so you understand the problem of feeding these snakes.

The best but not perfect solution is to provide the snake with a diet based on chicken eggs. Open a fresh egg at one end, pour it into a bowl, and mix it with about the same amount of water. Add a few drops of a liquid vitamin and calcium supplement, and put about a third of the mixture back into the egg shell. Refrigerate the remaining mix. Place the loaded egg (with an opening large enough for the snake to enter with its head) into the scarlet snake terrarium at night, when the snake is most likely to be active. Wedge it into place to prevent too much egg mix from spilling. With luck, the scarlet snake will smell the egg and suck out its contents. Try this feeding method every other night and hope for the best. Some specimens feed well after one or two attempts, some take the egg mix reluctantly about once a month, and some never feed in captivity at all. Hobbyists

Texas Rarity

One of the rarest North American snakes is the Texas scarlet snake, *Cemophora coccinea lineri*, named after Louisiana herpetologist Ernie Liner. Few specimens have been found, and even fewer have been kept by hobbyists. The Texas scarlet snake can been seen only in a narrow strip along the southeastern coast of Texas from north of Brownsville to the Laguna Madre area, This range is separated by many miles from the range of other scarlet snakes, so the Texas Scarlet Snake might be a full species. It is completely protected by the state of Texas.

An example of the extremely rare Texas scarlet snake.

have even tried to add very finely chopped mouse flesh to the mix in an attempt to wean the snake over to a mouse diet, but this seldom works. If you can get the snake to feed once a month, it should survive. Captive reproduction, as you might expect, has been rare. If a successful egg laying occurs, the four to eight eggs can be incubated just like milk-snake eggs.

Sonoran Mountain Kingsnake, *Lampropeltis pyromelana*

One of the most brightly colored of the tricolored kingsnakes, Sonoran mountain kings are milksnakes in almost everything but the name. They are slender snakes that are typically 20 to 30 inches long, rarely reaching 40 inches, and they are covered with glistening rings of bright red, clean black, and solid white. The rings cross the belly, though the black rings often are reduced in size there. Colors seldom darken as the snakes mature. In all forms, the snout is bright white, that there are black caps over the eyes. The Sonoran mountain kingsnakes have more rows of scales around midbody than do milksnakes (twenty-one to twenty-three versus nineteen to twenty-one) and more white bands (thirty-one to sixty versus fewer than thirty in milk-snakes). The species occurs as several scattered and isolated forms (often called subspecies) at higher elevations from Utah and Nevada through Arizona and New Mexico and into northern Mexico. A Mexican subspecies, *L. p. knoblochi*, the Chihuahuan mountain kingsnake, is perhaps more readily available to hobbyists than are specimens from the United States.

Not only is this a beautiful species, but it is also relatively easy to keep for a small, slender snake. Most specimens do well at room temperatures between about 70 and 85 degrees Fahrenheit, and they don't need much additional undertank heating. A weak basking light should be used every day from spring into autumn.

In nature, the snakes live under rocks, fallen trees, and trash in pine and similar forests in the mountains, and they don't need high humidity. Design a relatively simple terrarium with rolls of pine bark as cover on a fairly absorbent substrate (aspen works well), and add a few bunches of pine needles for a natural touch. Because they bask frequently, Sonoran mountain kingsnakes are often out and easy to see, making them an excellent display species.

They are active snakes that take small mice without complaint. Suit the size of the mouse to the width of the snake's

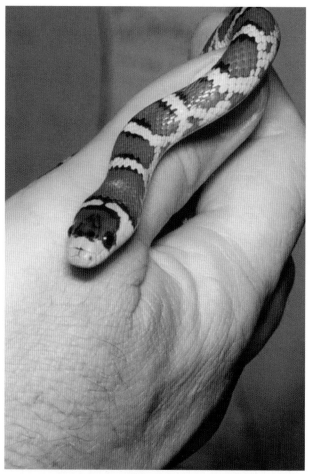

The Sonoran mountain kingsnake could double for a milksnake in both looks and maintenance requirements.

head, ranging from pinkies for hatchlings to hoppers for adults. Most specimens will take freshly killed or frozen and thawed mice. Remember that live mice must never be left unsupervised with any snakes. For their first few meals, some hatchlings insist on lizard-scented pinkies or pinky parts. Breeding is common in the terrarium, taking place in the spring after three or four months of lowered temperatures (allow the terrarium to drop to 55 to 60 degrees Fahrenheit). Three to six large, elongated eggs are typically laid and hatch in about two months. Treat them much as you would milk-snake eggs and expect a fair amount of success.

Resources

Center for North American Herpetology
This internet site, http://www.cnah.org, calls itself the "Academic Portal to North American Herpetology" and deserves the name. Here, you will find a comprehensive checklist of North American herps, photos of many, information on all aspects of herpetology, and free PDFs of many scientific papers.

Kingsnake.com
Kingsnake.com provides a portal to commercial suppliers and breeders around the world. It also includes access to the latest laws in all the states and countries as they apply to snakes and other herps, as well as links to many other aspects of the herp hobby.

Reptilechannel.com
Sponsored by *REPTILES* magazine, http://reptilechannel.com is an interesting site with much basic information about all types of reptiles and amphibians and the herp hobby. Check it for breeder listings and the latest herp news, including lists of upcoming reptile expos and local reptile shows across the United States.

Bibliography

Bartlett, R. D., and A. Tennant. *Snakes of North America: Western Region.* Houston: Gulf Publications, 2000.

Conant, R., and J. T. Collins. *A Field Guide to Reptiles and Amphibians: Eastern and Central North America.* Boston: Houghton Mifflin, 1998.

Markel, R. G. *Kingsnakes and Milk Snakes.* Neptune City, N.J.: T.F.H. Publications, 1990.

Pyron, R. A., and F. T. Burbink. "Neogene Diversification and Taxonomic Stability in the Snake Tribe Lampropeltini (Serpentes: Colubridae)." *Molecular Phylogenetics and Evolution* 52 (2009): 524–529.

Rossi, J. V. *Snakes of the United States and Canada: Keeping Them Healthy in Captivity*, vol. 1, *Eastern Area.* Malabar, Fla.: Krieger Publications, 1992.

_____, and R. Rossi. *Snakes of the United States and Canada. Keeping Them Healthy in Captivity*, vol. 2, *Western Area.* Malabar, Fla.: Krieger Publications, 1995.

Tennant, A. *Snakes of North America. Eastern and Central Regions.* Lanham, Md.: Lone Star Books, 2003.

Walls, J. G. *Gray-Banded Kingsnakes: Identification, Care, and Breeding.* Neptune City, N.J.: T.F.H. Publications, 1996.

_____. *Vivaria Designs.* Advanced Vivarium Systems. Irvine, Calif.: BowTie Press, 2007.

Williams, K. L. *Systematics and Natural History of the American Milksnake*, Lampropeltis Triangulum, 2nd ed. Milwaukee, Wis.: Milwaukee Public Museum, 1988.

Index

D

defection. *See* feces
diapers, 63
diseases and disorders
  about, 102–3
  mites, 33, 35, 40, 49, 103–4
  mouthrot, 104–5
  quarantine as preventive
    measure, 35–36, 106
  record keeping, 106–7
  shedding problems, 105
  URIs, 105
  See also bacteria
DNA testing of species, 10–13

E

eastern milksnake (*L. t.*
  triangulum), 66–67, 74
egg box, 88
egg laying and care of eggs, 88–89
egg tooth, 89
emergency kit, 105
enclosures, home-built, 40–41. *See*
  also housing your milksnakes
environmental niches in the wild, 18
equipment
  bowls for water, 47–48
  diapers, 63
  emergency kit, 105
  incubator, 89
  for misting, 41
  sexing probe, 81
  snake hooks, 61
  See also housing your milk-
    snakes
estivation period, 19
Extenuata group, 12
eyecaps, 105

F

family reaction to milksnakes, 23
fasting periods, 58
feces
  record keeping, 107
  removing from enclosure, 45, 51
  as signal for feeding, 56
  in water bowls, 48
feeding your milksnakes
  amounts, 56
  fasting periods, 58

feeding times, 55–56
food types, 53–55
hatchlings, 29, 57, 58, 90–91
picky eaters, 56–58
prehibernation, 82–83
pushing for breeding program,
  79
supplements, 58–59
females
  distinctions from males, 19, 80
  pregnancy, 86–88
  storing sperm, 96
fiberglass terraria, 39–40
Fitzinger, Leopold, 9
food types, 53–55
frozen rodents, 53, 54–55, 56, 58
full-spectrum lighting, 46
fuzzy mice, 54

G

genetics and taxonomy, 10–13
genus, species, and subspecies
  classifications, 7–9. *See also*
    taxonomy
Getula group, 12
glass aquaria, 38–39
glossy snakes (*Arizona*), 11, 93–94
gopher snakes (*Pituophis*), 11, 99
gravid (pregnant) females, 86–88
gray-banded kingsnake (*L.
  alterna*), 22, 112

H

habitat and range, 15–18, 38, 41,
  57, 83–84. *See also* milksnakes as pets
habits, 18–19, 62
handling eggs, 89
handling milksnakes, 60–63
hatchlings
  about, 19–20, 89–90
  feeding, 29, 57, 58, 90–91
  health, checking for, 32–33,
    102–3
heat sources, 41, 42–44
heaters, 43
heating pads, 42, 43
hemipenes, 19, 80
herp shows, 32
hibernation, 82–86